THE
SILVER SNARLING
TRUMPET

THE SILVER SNARLING TRUMPET

THE BIRTH OF THE GRATEFUL DEAD

THE LOST MANUSCRIPT OF
ROBERT HUNTER

hachette
BOOKS

New York

Hachette Books
Hachette Book Group
1290 Avenue of the Americas
New York, NY 10104
HachetteBooks.com
Twitter.com/HachetteBooks
Instagram.com/HachetteBooks

First Edition: October 2024

Published by Hachette Books, an imprint of Hachette Book Group, Inc. The Hachette Books name and logo is a trademark of the Hachette Book Group.

The Hachette Speakers Bureau provides a wide range of authors for speaking events. To find out more, go to hachettespeakersbureau.com or email HachetteSpeakers@hbgusa.com.

Books by Hachette Books may be purchased in bulk for business, educational, or promotional use. For information, please contact your local bookseller or Hachette Book Group Special Markets Department at special.markets@hbgusa.com.

The publisher is not responsible for websites (or their content) that are not owned by the publisher.

Print book interior design by Amy Quinn.

Library of Congress Control Number: 2024939750

ISBNs: 978-0-306-83515-5 (hardcover), 978-0-306-83517-9 (ebook)

Printed in the United States of America

LSC-C

Printing 1, 2024

CONTENTS

ACKNOWLEDGMENTS

ROBERT STARTED WRITING *THE SILVER SNARLING TRUMPET* LATE in his nineteenth year and into his twenties, he often spoke about those formative years in Palo Alto and the young people you'll meet in this book with great fondness.

When we married in 1982 and soon after moved house, Robert put a bunch of his writings (including the original manuscript for this book) into a large trunk and into our storage unit not to be rediscovered until last year, when interest in making a film about that period came to my attention. It occurred to me that perhaps *The Silver Snarling Trumpet*'s time had come to be shared.

It's a genuine piece of history and a glimpse into a time period that would set the foundations for everything that followed. What struck me when reading the book is how cognizant these young people were that they were a part of something important, a cultural shift that was fast approaching—the crossroads between the beatnik generation and the birth of the burgeoning San Francisco music scene, an exciting time that Robert faithfully documented in these pages. It makes me very happy that it is now being published and enjoyed.

I would like to thank Brant Rumble and all the wonderful people at Hachette Books, Mary Ann Naples, Michelle Aielli,

Acknowledgments

Michael Barrs, Amanda Kain, Sharon Kunz, Monica Oluwek, Cisca Schreefel, Amy Quinn, and Mollie Weisenfeld.

Special thanks to Steve Martin, Jeff Rosen, and David Rosenthal, who made this happen, and to John Mayer, Dennis McNally, and my dearest friend Brigid Meier for writing the pieces for the book.

Maureen Hunter

FOREWORD
~BY JOHN MAYER~

WHEN I WAS ASKED TO WRITE A FOREWORD TO A newly unearthed manuscript written by Robert Hunter, I immediately said yes. I knew that anything that came from his mind would interest me. Looking back on it, I suppose I was semiprepared to read something abstract and to search for the messages where they might be hiding. After all, historically, lost works of art tend to help explain why they might have been shelved in the first place. Time bears out the best of the unpublished, and, eventually, all that remains are high hopes and some assemblages of fits and starts.

It was around the very first page of this book that I realized that was not the case, and that I was holding one of the most important documents in Robert Hunter's—and Grateful Dead's—history. A lost box of film that, when developed, would reveal some of the most striking images you've ever seen, the kind that make you go slack-jawed and your heart race. What you're holding in your hands is not a recollection or a reconstruction. It is not a sifting through the sands of time to reach the long out of touch; it is a journal of the coming of age of one of the greatest lyricists the modern music world has ever known, and, at times, his friend, a young man known simply as "Jerry." It is also a stark, deeply sensory account of the early

1960s that is brought to life so tactilely that, at times, it's hard to believe you're not peering through a viewfinder.

History can only hold on to so much, and so it's usually the big shiny things that fit neatly into easily digestible timelines that it recalls, when all the while we know there was more—the seemingly insignificant car rides and the late-night talks and the countless times when nothing happened, except the slow and steady internal formation of a brilliance that would go on to change the world. We also know that these memories belong solemnly to the artists, until they drift away from their own grasp as well.

For decades, Deadheads have considered the story told, at least by its originators. Their interpretation might evolve, but the words in the story, they've dried on the page. Passionate followers of this music have learned to make the most of what was so generously given, reconstructing the dream through music, lyrics, photos, and anecdotes. Through the collective work of millions, they have pieced together a scale model of a dream that, in reality, was shared by six or eight or ten young men beginning in the early 1960s.

Our dreams of this music were Robert Hunter's life experiences, before all the years combined, as he would later go on to write. They are both milestone and mundane, and sometimes we the reader take on the task of separating one from the other, and perhaps seeing the big in the small, and vice versa. Where nothing happens, everything happens within; there is no moment too oblique, no sense too slight, not to investigate with the sharp and playful poetic mind that we would come to know years later through Hunter's lyrics. It's always surprising to me that even while the timbre is developing, the artistic voice is always there, no matter how early you go back. These stories are spoken in a very familiar rhythm—the swirl of the fingerprint is already deeply set.

And so, as keepers of the story, both young and old, whether Deadheads with fifteen years under their belt (me) or sixty, this is something new to us all: the great reveal of the early days of what would become the duo of Robert Hunter and Jerry Garcia, arguably the greatest songbook in American history, and a band called Grateful Dead. But all icons begin as people, and all art begins as their sensation of the world around them, and this is a deeply personal account of both. We have always considered ourselves lucky to be given so much through the words and music, and today, we have gotten even luckier. This is a gift—a rare, special, and important hand-drawn blueprint by the architect of the dream himself. Discovering just a page of this book would have been enough to rejoice over. That we have hundreds is a reality I'm still trying to get my head around. Time itself has revealed something truly magnificent, and there is beauty to be found on every page.

INTRODUCTION
—BY DENNIS McNALLY—

A S THE GRATEFUL DEAD'S WIZARDLY, ICONIC LYRICIST, Robert Hunter created a mythic universe of stories in songs, an omni-dimensional America that included mountains, seas, deserts, and stars in their heavens. It was a nation of no fixed era or boundaries, populated by ramblers, gamblers, saints, wastrels, rogues, and visionaries (sometimes all in one character), cats (real and China), alligators, wolves, coal miners, judges, angels, fairies, locomotive engineers, soldiers, sailors, and the dying . . . among other things.

In 1962, at the age of twenty, he began work on a novel, a roman à clef titled *The Silver Snarling Trumpet*. In hindsight, it was a dry run, what his friend Brigid Meier called a launching pad for his life in words, although the form would change with practice. Later, he would observe that the subculture that would become known as the Grateful Dead began as a cluster of relationships long before there was a band; *Trumpet* is the story of that earliest community. As Dead Heads read this tale, they will come to realize that it is also the two-hundred-page version of the masterpiece lyric Hunter fashioned in the 1990s, "Days Between."

Robert Hunter was born Robert Burns in 1941 near San Luis Obispo, California. His family was sundered by his father's alcoholism, desertion, and a subsequent divorce, and Robert spent several years in a string of foster homes. The result, as he later put it, was that he "had probably more than the usual load of sensitive bullshit as a young man."

His life improved when his mother married Norman Hunter, a publishing executive. Robert adopted his stepfather's surname and learned from him: Norman would see the phrase "merciless north" in an essay and vividly mark Robert's life by hurling the paper across the room with the comment, "I don't ever want to see you attributing human attributes to nature again." Hunter laughed. "He busted me on the pathetic fallacy, which is the absolute *sine qua non* of the poor writer."

The immediate result of his improved writing was an F on a book report because the teacher said it was far too good for a seventh grader. Longer term, it was surely not accidental that just around this time, he began to write his first novel, a fifty-page handwritten fairy tale. He stuck with that self-image. Though he would concede as an adult that his gifts as a writer were more suited to lyrics than to prose, he would maintain that "I have a novelist's mentality." He began playing music at age nine, when his grandmother gave him a Hawaiian steel guitar, and in his teens, he picked up cello, violin, and trumpet.

The Hunters eventually settled in Palo Alto, where Robert attended high school for the tenth and eleventh grades. He joined the band and orchestra, the Free Thinkers Club ("the first I'd heard of atheism"), and the wrestling team, which gave him regular-guy credentials. In 1957, the family moved to Stamford, Connecticut, for his senior year and upended his circumstances. He resumed life as an outsider in a conservative, socially restrictive world, enlivened only by his first band, an old-fashioned combination of

Dixieland and rock and roll called the Crescents, for which he played trumpet.

After a semester at the University of Connecticut in the fall of 1958, useful only for learning about Pete Seeger and folk music, he returned to Palo Alto, was jilted by an old flame, enlisted in the National Guard, completed his initial tour of duty, and returned to Palo Alto in March 1961. Soon after his arrival, he attended a production of *Damn Yankees* at the Commedia Dell'arte there and an old friend introduced him to the volunteer lighting technician, a young proto-beatnik named Jerry Garcia. A day or two later, they met again at the local coffeehouse, Saint Michael's Alley. Along with Garcia's friend Alan Trist, a student from England taking a gap year before university, they began a conversation that would last their lifetimes.

Though he was only eighteen when they met, Garcia clearly had an outsize, charismatic personality that made him the center of their little group. A streetwise, intuitively nonconformist San Franciscan who had adopted Kerouac's *On the Road* as a life guide, he had talent as a painter, having studied with the well-known Beat assemblage artist Wally Hedrick at the San Francisco Art Institute, but he had shifted his focus to playing music. "He played the guitar anywhere from twenty-four to thirty-eight hours a day," Hunter wrote, "which would tend to be unnerving even if he were Segovia. However, he was *not* Segovia; he was Jerry. And the very act of being Jerry was, in his estimation, an excuse for almost anything."

Their group was rounded out by Trist, an eccentric fellow named Willy Legate, and a high school student named Barbara "Brigid" Meier.

Alan would later remark that "like any proper Englishman, I was a bit of a renegade." A literary intellectual who was up on

Rimbaud, Dylan Thomas, and the Beat bible, Don Allen's *New American Poetry*, Alan had even visited the legendary Beat Hotel in Paris. He was enthusiastic, stylish, and catalytic. Hunter would recall the thrill of absorbing "Howl" for the first time at Alan's, thinking "someone was going to bust in and arrest me for reading it."

Willy had a room that, along with his cigarette stash, he frequently shared with Hunter and Garcia. Legate was tall and stooped, with an enormous head, a bulging forehead, and thick glasses. Raised in Arkansas, he'd begun reading up on psychic research, the Rosicrucians, the theosophist Annie Besant, and yoga in high school, and while in college in 1959, he learned how to cadge vials of LSD from the manufacturer.

He never, wrote Hunter, "said a great deal, or if he did, it was mainly incomprehensible." He "could always be found at one extreme pole or the other, politically, mentally, and Willy-wise." Mostly, he responded to questions with "Won't tell ya." Years later, Garcia reflected that "we all learned how to think a certain kind of way from Willy . . . things that come out of sequence—nonlinear, Zen, synchronistic thinking. How to think funny, the cosmic laugh." Hunter concluded, "Willy was the kind of person who somehow made you wonder just who *you* were, where you were going, and if maybe he didn't have the right idea after all."

Brigid Meier was their precocious younger sister, beautiful and at least as well read as the rest—and eager to learn more. A budding intellectual, artist, and poet, she had, as she recently wrote, "a healthy dose of rabid anti-authoritarianism combined with a sense of the absurd; we knew we didn't belong to the dominant culture of consumerism and conformity." In 1962, she wrote a poem about them all; she was "in rapture of the thing / where we are all in love / with Life / and each other." She was their spiritual glue.

Finally, there was Hunter, who Brigid's poem called "the blind man" with his glasses, the observer. Garcia would assess Hunter's depiction of people in *Trumpet* as generally quite accurate, except for his portrayal of himself, which he tends to omit. His subject is their scene, which they were all preternaturally aware of as being special. They roamed from their "library," Kepler's Books, where they read and talked (and where the kindly owner protected them despite their penury), to their hangout at the coffeehouse, to the Felliniesque parties at places like the boardinghouse known as the Chateau.

It was a scene, Hunter recorded, where "love was the essence of it, and a sense of kinship touched each of us . . . though it is the sort of thing that cannot quite withstand the harsh light of scrutiny." Alan saw it as well. "And then there's a love thing," he added. "We all feel it sometimes, but we're afraid to say it, and sometimes we wish we'd said it when it's too late to. When you suddenly realize how close you came to losing your last chance, or how suddenly you might lose it, it's time to start reworking your values."

One reason for their intimate connection was the car accident a month before that had blown Garcia out of his shoes and through the windshield, cost Alan an inch of height through a back injury, and killed their friend Paul Speegle, whose art had impressed them.

"That's how this group really began . . . I mean, as more than a social clique," Hunter recorded Jerry as saying. "A lot of us seemed to realize this and it drew us closer together. It all happened just before you [Hunter] came around. You missed the game, but you got the score, though. That's the thing that counts in the end." The accident, and the fact that he had survived—and that Speegle had not—made Garcia "realize that I could never be sure where I'd be tomorrow, or even if I'd be alive. That's why I'm living like I am now, doing what I want to do instead of working away at some job to establish the security for a tomorrow I might never be around to see."

Their attitudes were not at all political—"If the truth be known," Hunter wrote, "with a few exceptions (notably Willy), our collective political knowledge and views were next to nonexistent. Besides being positively anti-HUAC (as who wasn't), anti-bomb (we had our own personal interests to consider), and anti–present administration (as who, in the history of mankind, hasn't been?), we more or less didn't give a collective damn about such goings-on in general."

Instead, they were consciously anti-consumer. Hunter ranted on the subject: "Daddy, security blanket, and God; an air-conditioned, employer-employee relationshipped, wage-scaled holy trinity with 5 percent of your yearly earnings in the form of a Christmas Bonus masquerading as the Virgin Mary."

"We were different from other human creatures and knew it; reveled in it." Hunter depicted them singing as they strolled down the street, which would lead people to "avert their eyes as though afraid to admit the presence of such an enormous breach of etiquette . . . the same people who would pause for minutes to observe the twisted metal and broken glass of an automobile accident. But then, an auto wreck was more socially acceptable than we were."

Their scene was a part of the bridge from Beat to hippie. As such, Hunter wrote later, *Trumpet* was a "representative artifact of the dawn of the sixties." They knew something was happening, but they didn't yet know quite what it was . . . so they waited. "While we were waiting, we learned one another, for this was a time when all guards were down and pretention was ridiculous on its face, except in jest. Guards were down, but never the faith of the true believer . . . at least not in the conviction that 'it' would one day walk through that very door."

The book's title is a quotation from John Keats's "The Eve of St. Agnes," a celebration of romantic love that begins with a man about to die. It gave Hunter his identity as a writer, and in the years to come, he would fully earn the label.

Though he had a reputation for contrarianism—and it was definitely inadvisable to ask him about the meaning of his songs—Hunter's treatment of me as the band's historian was kindness in itself, including lending me his copy of *The Silver Snarling Trumpet* early in the 1980s as I began research. It was a gold mine of information, capturing not only events but attitudes and atmospheres. His gift for deep understanding and expression, something he later called his ability to describe hallucinations, is already on display in the novel, as is his ear for speech and his sharp wit.

There's a scene in which they sit in Saint Michael's Alley and discuss a play they're writing together. "The dialogue's beginning to drag a little," Trist said, "so we've decided to write in the eruption of Mount Vesuvius for act twelve." Then he described how amid decadence and enough action for ten normal plays, a small black beetle at center stage would contemplate the eternal truths until, about to utter them, it would be flattened by an elephant.

"We expect to run through several beetles in rehearsals," Garcia admitted.

"The essential strategy will be to charge no admission but lock the doors and charge a fee to get out," concluded Alan.

They could be wonderfully silly, taking alliterative wordplay into the stratosphere, "fertile feliciousness of your prehensile predilection." Or, when stoned, they decided that the typewriter in the room had legs, which elicited Alan's comment, "Nothing but run-on sentences, horrible . . . horrible." Humor was at the core of their love for one another.

Hunter also makes an honest historian, describing his brief career of singing with Garcia ("Bob and Jerry") before Garcia moved on, reminding Robert, "You've got your writing . . . singing is a pastime for you."

Late in 1961, Trist returned to England. None of them were great correspondents, but nine years later, he would return to California to join the Dead. Before he left, they gathered again to walk around San Francisco. On that walk, "the love scene had seen fit to reappear for a few moments, that was all. Only this time, there was no talk, no heralds, no sense of tingling anticipation surrounding her visit. On a morning in San Francisco, after a small party, traveling down an unfamiliar street at early dawn, she had found us, and she looked the same as always."

Hunter and Garcia and the rest of the Grateful Dead would spend the succeeding decades creating a love scene that would flourish beyond all expectations. *The Silver Snarling Trumpet* is the first blossom of the many flowers that were to come.

The silver, snarling trumpets 'gan to chide:

. . .

The music, yearning like a God in pain.

—*John Keats, "The Eve of St. Agnes"*

AUTHOR'S NOTE

I'VE JUST READ THE MANUSCRIPT OF THIS BOOK FOR THE FIRST time, twenty years, or nearly so, after writing it. The events detailed occurred in my nineteenth and twentieth years, and it was written immediately after the last scene occurred and was my major occupation for the following year.

Although the last chapter speaks of the breakup of the scene, many of the "hard core" herein described are still functioning together, so it was not as easy to dismiss as all that, prophet of melancholy as I was.

Some of the characterizations are shallow, and I gave myself the last word on subjects several times, which I may not have had. Jerry Garcia once said that I got everyone down with some degree of accuracy in the book, except myself. Some of the characters, notably Rudolph Jackson, the sad trumpet player who wanders in and out of the story, are accurate to a T; others, such as David X., are given short shrift with a couple of lines not indicating their actual bearing on the scene.

I made one bad error in composition, in that I felt the first draft was too short to make a respectable book, so I rewrote it, waxing eloquent whenever possible, which explains a lot of the extraneous and repetitive philosophizing that mar the book, much of it being downright trite. However, to change it or delete it would be a disservice to the twenty-year-old mind that conceived it, and whose book it is, scarcely mine.

Not to write my own review (and then he does), but I think there is a value in the book I scarcely dreamed of when writing it. It occurs to me that it is a representative artifact of the dawn of the sixties and that the attitudes and experiences we had were being more or less duplicated here and there about the country in an era best designated post-Beat and pre-hippie. Pot was extremely scarce, and LSD had not yet appeared. Bennies were rare, but sometimes we scored thirty or forty and abused them mightily till we ran out. Coffee and wine made do. It gives me a certain pride to note that our "scene" did not evolve from getting stoned: that came somewhat later, with mixed blessings.

We were the first front of "war babies" hitting the streets for the first time. Roy Kepler and the staff at his bookstore in Menlo Park allowed us to exist in an intellectual atmosphere with a built-in library. People heard there was a scene and fell by; the periphery of our social life extended to hundreds of bright, interesting folks from Stanford, the surrounding community, and the flowering local electronics industry.

I don't plead the book as a piece of good writing, that is as may be, and my ego is pretty disinvolved after two decades, but as a singular curiosity whose value is wholly unintentional on the part of the writer.

I feel apologetic to those I failed to mention, especially Karl Moore, who was angry at not being included, but figured it made no difference since it was the worst book ever written anyway.

I have no intentions of ever publishing this record, being content to preserve it as an "archive item" whose chief value will be to refresh my memory of what I was about every couple of decades, and to serve as source material for those with time and energy to construct a more complete picture of these and subsequent events.

Robert Hunter, June 19, 1982

THE
SILVER SNARLING
TRUMPET

With reverence adorn thine acts and face,
That he may delight to speed us up the mount;
Think that it dawns but once, this day of grace.

—Dante, Purgatorio, Canto XII

For Darjeeling

PREFACE

"AND SO?" WELL, THAT SEEMS TO BE THE ULTIMATE QUES-tion itself. To the novice weaver, the transition from pattern to tapestry must be fraught with the same uncertainty; will the work, when completed, be worth the money expended for materials, or the time patiently spent over the loom? Each man, it appears, has his Dantean path, replete with his personal leopards, lions, and she-wolves, each dedicated to the life-long task of chasing him from the road that seems to lead so surely to the all-encompassing light. Consequently, he often loses himself in the forest by the way; the paths and hiding places of which the beasts know so much better than he; or finds himself running to a modern-day Daniel with a PhD to find out why he runs from that which pursues him (or to be convinced, while the beast pants at his heels, that he is not being fazed at all).

There is no time of life so ripe for gathering the fruits of experience as that indecisive time which occurs before turning off the side path of youth onto the highway that parallels it. It is a time when the highway, with its awesome promise, lies just across the way, but the No Trespassing signs keep one from cutting across the ripening meadows that offer an alluring shortcut. Both roads seem to stretch to infinity, winding through forests and beside rivers . . . some mighty and some insignificant. The test, in the end, is not of being on the more resplendent highway but of the method by which the transition is accomplished, if ever.

Some never complete the transition, and you can see many of them hopping off the freight trains outside Los Angeles in order to escape the clutches of the "Bulls" who lie in wait for them, clubs poised, in the railroad yards . . . that eternal haunt of the uncertain path, the man who is waiting to trip you up when you're not doing nobody no harm, just living your life.

Some make the cross too quickly and uneventfully to ever completely appreciate that which lies around the turns and in the ditches that run beside the highway; too quickly to ever savor the lingering shadows with which it can tint the memory. Memory, after all, is what endures when all the beautiful groves along the road have been enjoyed and all the enticing caves explored.

We exist not in the future, nor in the past, but in that precise, unmeasurable point of time that rushes headlong into the next point and is called the present. Memory is that intangible concept that fits these "instants" into a continuum. A motion picture may be stopped in the middle of an action, and that which is occurring on the film will be captured, immobile, upon the screen. The picture thus held contains an infinity of the aforementioned "instants" (not even considering the rest of the reel, since infinity can be added to and subtracted from and still remain infinity, by its very nature; or so I was informed by a mathematically inclined acquaintance). What has already been projected upon the screen is memory, what is to come is future; what is retained upon the screen is a mixture of past and future, except for one infinitely minute point, which is *present*.

It goes against the venerable spirit of "Zen" to try to stop the picture in our lives. 'Tis not only "un-Zen" but impossible . . . this way dwells madness or, at least, mild frustration.

Somewhere along the road is the point at which one must cross over or continue forever kicking up dust along the primary path. For some, it is a painful crossing, for others an exuberant sort of sad joy. It is a youth that has suddenly been brought face-to-face with the concept of losing youth (a cognition that one must assimilate before transition is possible). Frightening, but altogether necessary.

There is no end to the journey short of senility (which has stopped at a convenient spot . . . sometimes a warm, shaded grove; sometimes a granite rock exposed to the merciless beating of the sun) or death, an end to all roads, or perhaps the beginning of another.

The ending of this tale is only the finis of a "stage." "Stages!" . . . the ever-recurrent bends in the road that must eventually lead to where the road builder paused in the inviting shade of a roadside nook to look back upon what he had done. Impressed with the Herculean task he had taken on, he paused longer than he expected, so inviting was the rest, and there may still be found, lost in reflection.

Even the Methuselah must eventually find his nook.

Look up and down that long lonesome road,
Where all your friends have gone, my lord,
Where you and I must go.

Look up and down that long lonesome road,
Hang down your head and cry, poor boy,
Hang down your head and cry.

—Trad. Folk

MENLO PARK, 1961. IT IS ON SUMMER DAYS WITH TIME on my hands and little or nothing to do that I remember other summer days with time on my hands. It was a different *sort* of time; the sort of time over which the years hang gaudy veils, making them appear much brighter than perhaps they were. But that's a good thing really. A man's *now* is often such an overpowering collection of effects from causes but dimly remembered that bygone days must occasionally fan the forge . . . if only to convince him that his blade was ever truly tempered to do the sizable job of carving set before him. What is a man's mind, after all is said and done, but a collection of memories . . . and what is his present but a collection of infinitely tiny points of *now* whose value, in the end, must be measured in terms of what memory, the eventual edifice of which is his character?

I think that I began to realize this somewhere back in a certain conglomeration that has its existence now only as a pleasant chuckhole somewhere in my brain. Strange to think back on those days when it was perfectly natural that we all slept on the floor in one small room . . . and woke up wanting cigarettes that none of us had, so we passed around the few decent-sized butts that had collected in the fishbowl, remnants of more plentiful times, then went out on early-morning excursions along mist-dampened streets to find more.

It was an impressive room, half again as big as a closet and generally filled to overflowing with loose papers, trash, smoke, people, and other paraphernalia. Half of it was dominated by a makeshift bed, which would uncomfortably sleep anywhere from one to seven people (except when there were more). Most of the other half was occupied by a desk constructed from boards and orange crates. In the two or three square feet of remaining space was our ballroom . . . the center of parties and other recreations such as are occasionally good for the mind and spirit.

These were the days before practical considerations, matters of "importance," began to eat our minds. We were all poets and philosophers then, until we began to wonder why we had so few concrete worries and went out to look for some. We of the small room were fairly sure that we understood the solutions to the problems of the world, so we took a few of those problems on our shoulders only to find out, too late, that it didn't make any difference if we knew the solutions or not; up close, the problems changed, and we with them, and suddenly we were caught, inextricably, in the midst of things. So we grew up, the way we'd been being urged to all along, and assumed a mature viewpoint.

Most of us had little other than the clothes we somehow happened to have come by, and if they happened to stick to us, it wasn't a matter for serious worry because really, you know, that's the way things were, and things like that don't bother you too much unless you have some sort of strange idea that it *should*.

It was the *people* who made the "scene" revolve; wonderful, inexhaustible people we thought . . . until we began to question things that perhaps we ought not to have questioned, things such as "Can we live this way forever?" Perhaps we could have if we hadn't asked, but by the very act of becoming conscious that a question existed, an answer became imperative. Part of the answer seemed to lie in the realm of whatever it was that society demanded of us . . . and what it demanded was our lives. Given impetus by this snatch of what seemed to be an answer, we began to ask the question of one another, and from there, it was only a small step to becoming frightened. And that, of course, was the end of being carefree, for we had begun, if only by the act of questioning, to care.

Others came along, others who would have belonged with us before, except that we began to question them too. Not seeing fit to acknowledge that such a question existed, they took over our philosophy and our guitars, our beards and cigarette butts, and left us with the world.

I remember coffeehouses and empty pockets, the unplanned, unending parties . . . the bad wine, the music that is inseparable from the impoverished decadence, and wonder sometimes if it was a fair trade.

THE DAY WAS BEAUTIFUL, AS USUAL. THEY HAD BEEN OCCURRING as regularly as clockwork, the kind of days that make you feel generally dissatisfied because you know you should be outside taking advantage of them while they last, instead of sitting in the coffeehouse. As I sat staring out the window, it occurred to me that probably everyone fancies himself a connoisseur of nature, but many are probably secretly pleased when a foul day comes along and they don't have to frantically run around proving it to themselves.

It seemed to me that there was something essentially hypocritical about staying inside when balmy weather calls, even though it *is* more comfortable, and perhaps this was one of the secret keys to the paranoia of our day.

Merely realizing this fact did not ease my conscience, so I paid for my coffee (I was a penny short, so I left what I had on the counter) and determinedly stalked out to damn well enjoy the sunshine.

I walked slowly up the avenue trying to decide on a destination. As I threaded my way through midafternoon shoppers, I became conscious of myself as part of a massive bidirectional flow of essentially directionless humanity. It seemed as though it might be pleasant to just drift with them, with no goal in mind. I tried it for a few minutes, but, as interesting and Zen as the idea sounded, it wasn't really much fun, so I decided to hell with it and started to walk home.

The flow seemed definitely averse to going in my direction and tried to hustle me back toward the coffeehouse. I fought my way wholeheartedly through the river of conglomerated flesh. One trod-upon-toe glowered at me as though I were going the wrong way on a one-way street (which is fundamentally the wrong thing to do, you know, even though it's often the most direct means to one's destination). I replied with a faint, all-purpose "Eat it, Charlie" smile and continued unswerving until I reached the highway.

It was a good twenty loose-shoe-sole-flapping-minute walk from downtown, and the sun had begun to tingle at the back of my neck by the time I got to the room. When I opened the door, the accumulated heat rolled over me like a wave. The closed windows successfully warded off any stray breeze that might have been knocking about. I hit two of them sharply with the heel of my hand and felt a faint, unsatisfactory draft wander in uncertainly as they banged open. I knocked open another one, still to no avail, and banged futilely at the two that opened only on whim, their good pleasure, at the moment, being to remain aloof.

The room was deserted except for myself and the Blind Prophet. The Blind Prophet was the lord and protector of the room, entrusted with the spiritual well-being of his easily tempted charges who occupied the room along with myself. He abided in an unframed canvas that always managed to hang slightly askew on the wall.

Against a somber background of swirling blacks, the sightless eyes of the Prophet kept vigil over the room. The artist had died tragically, a few weeks before I had arrived on the scene, in an automobile accident. His memory was revered highly by my comrades, and although I had not known him, at times, I could almost sense that he looked out of the sightless eyes over the lives of the people of whom he had been an integral part.

Often at night, with a dim light burning in the corner, I had watched his cavernous hollows as I drifted off to sleep. At times, they were frightening and accusative; more often, they radiated a warming comfort. They were unfathomable but held promise of great secrets to be learned if one should watch them long enough.

I pulled off my decrepit shoes and lay down on the monstrous bed. The midday heat of the room was oppressive and dulling to the senses. It was rendered more irritating still by the pungent odor of moist instant coffee emanating from an uncapped jar. I pondered getting up and putting the cap back on the jar, but the pondering exhausted the last bit of my energy. As my mind grew duller, I wondered idly if the fumes would asphyxiate me, then decided that I was *more* likely to die of heat prostration if I were to stand up. My eyes wandered around the room, fixing on the Blind Prophet as they closed.

Colors played through my mind, wafted by imaginary heat waves. I tried to picture an iceberg from the pinpoints of color and had succeeded in massing them into a bluish-white flame just as a fly made a three-point on my upper lip. I brushed him away and heard him buzz frantically around the room. I knew he'd be back in a few seconds . . . flies always seem to sense when you're in a defenseless position. I waited patiently for a few seconds. The buzzing stopped. Perhaps he'd flown out the window . . . no, that was too incredible to believe, not with me at his mercy. As I waited, the colors began to overtake me, hesitantly.

I had a dream that came back to me several days later with remarkable clarity. I found myself in a glass case, suspended in space. The walls were of a brilliant, crystal quality. The sunlight pierced through the sides and projected a spectrum of prismatic colors on the arid plane below me. The ground seemed to absorb the colors, for I noticed them growing dimmer and dimmer as I watched.

A tripod seemed to grow out of the plane right in front of me. It was the only object that marred the smoothness of the plane . . . a completely flat desertlike plane that stretched as far as my eye could see. An easel rested on the tripod, but no canvas.

I suddenly became aware of a man who seemed to be walking toward the tripod. He walked slowly and seemed to be meditating very hard. When he reached the tripod, he looked at it as though surprised to find it there. He stood very still for a while. He had a gray face that seemed to be molded, badly, from a lump of clay. His eyes shifted suspiciously around in his misshapen skull, then fixed themselves on the easel. He surveyed it for a moment and took off his coat. Then he removed his soul, forcing his rubbery mouth open with gray, grotesquely gnarled fingers and vomiting it onto the easel. He stretched the soul over the easel, securing it with pins.

He stepped back and studied it, then picked up a palette that hung on the easel and dipped his tongue into the paint. He licked a streak of dull red paint across the easel, then stepped back again and looked at it critically.

"Red . . . I am passion," I heard him say. He again dipped his tongue into the paint, drooling it onto the easel. "Gold . . . I am beauty!" then, "Green . . . I am a lover of nature."

He selected again. "Purple . . . I am grandeur," then, "Blue . . . I am sorrow, for the world is not as it should be."

When he had finished, he stepped away from the easel and looked at what he had done. Satisfied, he unpinned his soul from the easel and swallowed it, then put on his coat. From my vantage point, I saw him walk slowly across the plane until he was out of sight. When I looked back, another man had appeared before the easel. He stood uncertainly for a moment, peering suspiciously about him, then removed his coat.

I watched from my crystal cage, suspended in space . . . Suddenly, I realized that my cage had become an oven. The sides began to lose their transparency as they grew red with heat. Completely incongruous strains of music drilled into my mind as I ran from wall to wall looking frantically for an escape from the heat.

When I awoke, my clothing was soaked with perspiration. The heat of the room was almost unbearable.

"Have a good nap?" Jerry asked. He had come in while I was asleep to practice his guitar.

"Who in hell shut the windows?"

"I did, obviously; it was too hot in here."

"So you shut the window . . . Where in hell did you learn *your* physics?"

"It's not a matter of physics, just common sense."

"Which alone should explain why it's beyond you."

I got up and opened a window. An overwhelming miasma of sun-ripened sewage from the bay fumed into the oven-like room before I could pull the window shut again. Jerry smiled victoriously and continued to play, his ill-combed, bearded head intent over his guitar.

He played the guitar anywhere from twenty-four to thirty-eight hours a day, which would tend to be unnerving even if he were Segovia. However, he was *not* Segovia; he was Jerry. And the very act of being Jerry was, in his estimation, an excuse for almost anything. He had the easygoing self-assurance of a person who is used to being forgiven for any gaucheness he might choose to perpetrate on his contemporaries, so he committed them with an amazing regularity and a completely innocent conscience. This attitude was made bearable only by virtue of the fact that it worked both ways; he, forgiving easily anything but innate "grossness" (mental or physical). "Gross" was Jerry's ultimate condemnation: a sin without possibility of intercession or forgiveness.

He was never known, in those days, to have a dollar in his pocket that could be attributed to work, but he had a facility for being taken care of that was better than money and was attested to by the fact that he never had a "lean and hungry look" about him. He was the stellar example of practical bohemianism, from the handwrought laurel wreaths that often graced his haggy mane, down to what one might expect to be cloven hooves, sheathed in incredibly aged socks. There was an essential joie de vivre in him that always lurked, Pan-like, behind his "something-the-cat-dragged-in" appearance. His philosophy of life was quite untenable, since he drastically changed it at least every three days to fit his particular frame of mind.

After finishing the song he was working on, he put down his fretted alarm clock. "Shall we thence away?"

"Whither?" I mumbled, still not fully recovered from my combination of dream, heat prostration, and nausea.

"I have a feeling that something's happening at the coffeehouse," he answered. Jerry always had a feeling that something was happening at the coffeehouse. Nothing bad ever happened there yet, to speak of, but when it did, Jerry certainly wanted to be there. The idea of something eventually happening there was as axiomatic in his mind as the implicit evil of grossness.

"Sounds all right."

"Want to take your car?"

I thought about it as I untied and replaced the shoes I had kicked off earlier and decided against it. Besides being brakeless and suffering from a host of other major infirmities, it was almost out of gas. Anyway, my license had been canceled for nonpayment of insurance. I was quite relieved, several weeks later, when somebody towed it away or stole it, lifting several thousand pounds of dead metal from my subconscious.

"Let's make it on foot."

"Why *not* take the car? . . . It's not doing us any good just sitting out there."

"Maybe it'll follow us over later if it feels neglected. We can save it a place at the table."

ALAN WAS SITTING BY HIMSELF WHEN WE WALKED IN. He looked up from his copy of Dylan Thomas's poetry and raised an eyebrow as we sat down. "And Death shall have no dominion!" he greeted us.

Alan was dressed, as usual, in Harris Tweed and a knit tie. He was sojourning in the colonies before beginning studies at Cambridge University and was having a rather fantastic time among the natives.

He automatically reached out to clear his pile of notebooks and paraphernalia, which he had spread over the small table, overturning his cup of coffee in one smooth action and apologizing profusely.

"You're the only man in the world who's so consistently clumsy . . . and with such innate grace," Jerry observed.

"We English are bred that way," Alan answered, trying vainly to stop the flood of coffee with a handful of paper napkins. Alan had a propensity for spilling things, bumping into chairs, knocking over lamps . . . all with perfect refinement and polish.

"How's the play coming along?" I asked.

"Well, we've got it down to nine hours and eighteen acts," Jerry answered.

"The dialogue's beginning to drag a little, so we've decided to write in the eruption of Mount Vesuvius for act twelve," Alan added. "Care for a preview of the first scene?"

"Well, not awfully."

"Oh, please," Jerry said, "don't deny us your critical facilities now . . . It might mean the birth of a new concept in drama."

"Well, I suppose . . ."

"Fine!" Alan said, and began to describe the setting.

"When the curtain rises, the audience sees two principal characters, Alexandroso and Cleotandra, reclining on vast chaise longues in a setting of complete and utter decadence. Several elephants are strewn at odd ends around the stage, ingesting the draperies, while an orchestra of four hundred recorders attempt to drown out the dialogue."

Jerry interrupted, "Most important is a small black beetle, elaborately robed so as to be seen from the audience, who resides center stage throughout the play, contemplating the eternal truths."

"Wasn't he hard to write dialogue for?" I inquired.

"Definitely," Alan answered, "but we took care of that. At the climax of the play, when it is about to utter the truths it has been contemplating, one of the elephants who has just finished eating the draperies crushes him."

"We expect to run through several beetles in rehearsals, but we figure that the ultimate goal . . . at its highest . . . justifies our means. Pragmatism, you know," Jerry added.

"As the action begins, Alexandroso reaches from his chaise and sounds a huge gong, signaling two eunuchs who come bounding in and light cigarettes for them with enormous torches. They each take one drag from the cigarettes, then crush them out upon the slaves' navels."

Jerry chuckled gleefully. "And in the meantime, the audience will be studying the copious footnotes, which will run to about nine twenty-pound volumes. We present these to them as they enter the theater so they can find out what in the hell's happening."

"Which will be nothing, of course?" I asked.

"Precisely."

Alan ordered a refill and, as the waiter filled his cup, proceeded with the dialogue. The waiter looked startled for a moment, then reassumed his detached face. "Far be it from me, my dear Alexandroso, to in any way perambulate perniciously in your presence, but it seems to me, insofar as it is within my power to ascertain, that that which is, in a word, preordained, might be harmonious with that which is not positively palpable to your perverse presence, or, in a word . . ."

Jerry continued, "My dear Cleotandra, I am considerably captivated by the conspicuous correlation of your capricious interpitude, but it seems to me that the vast vacuousness, related, insofar as it is within my excellent power to ascertain, appears to me, notwithstanding possible minor deviations to the contrary, which might seem to suggest . . ."

"You mean . . . ?"

"Precisely!"

"But my esteemable Alexandroso, we must realize the gargantuan . . . nay, *overwhelming* proclivity pendant, to a prodigious proportion, upon the productivity of parsimony, when derived in direct discord to diplomacy, must needs overwhelm that for which need has not been revitalized."

"Ah, but, my dear Cleotandra, you forget, nay . . . overlook, the aspect of gross retardation evident everywhere in minds that have not yet attained that astrological plane equivalent to our exalted level of intellect (they bow graciously to each other), and yet I humble myself to the fertile feliciousness of your prehensile predilection."

"And I to yours, my ambivalent acrophile."

"And now, my dear Cleotandra, here's my plan . . ."

"One moment, forsooth, my dear Alexandroso, here's my plan . . ."

"Allow me, my soporific seer, to interject a note of saturnine sobriety into your sagacious superciliousness; here's *my* plan . . ."

Alan concluded, "That should give you an idea of the dialogue. It will be widely varied, of course, except that every other act will be a repetition of the act immediately preceding."

"The essential strategy will be to charge no admission but lock the doors and charge a fee to get out."

"Except, of course, for those who do us the courtesy of staying for the whole performance. They get out for half price."

We had been gracing the establishment over Alan's single cup of coffee for about an hour, insidiously helping him drink his free refills, when a squat Negro shuffled in, wearing a green straw hat and carrying a trumpet slung over his shoulder in a pillowcase. He sat down at our table, his horn in his lap, and sighed heavily.

"How's it going, Jackson?" I asked mechanically. I regretted the question even as I felt the words leave my mouth.

"Ah, 'tis sad to relate, 'tis sad to relate," Jackson replied; obviously, the overture to a tale of pathos and woe such as this was an everyday occurrence with Jackson. He talked, as usual, to no one in particular, his eyes fastened upon some dim and distant horizon. He gave the vague impression of being a character out of some unrealistic book: unique, pathetic, despondent . . . in short, the perfect prototype, at twenty-six, of a classical misspent existence. Next to any and all women, he loved his horn. Neither seemed ever to return the favor. His horn was his constant companion, when out of hock. Whenever an occasion presented itself, he would essay to blow "soul," as it were, and the bane of his existence was the perpetual misanthrope who always appeared as soon as he got warmed up to say, "Hold it down for a while, man." When this happened, he would sit down, the one

27

true martyr of jazz, and discontentedly empty his spit valves for a half hour or so.

"What is it this time, Jack?" Jerry asked.

"Mmm—fickle womankind has once again thrust a dagger into this bleeding heart." He patted the battered brass of his trumpet affectionately through the pillowcase. "Shall I ever chance upon the wench whose fidelity approaches that of old 'Nellie Belle' here?"

There was some speculation that the reason for Jackson's perpetual despondency had its roots in his encounter with jazz trumpeter Miles Davis. Jackson had been sitting at the Jazz Workshop watching Davis perform, and had unobtrusively taken Nellie Belle out of its case during one of Davis's sets. He had waited patiently, blowing warm air through the horn until the set was over, then eased over to the bandstand and said, "Hey, babe, want to do something together?"

Davis had looked down (so it was reported by semi-reliable witnesses) and whispered loudly, "What you want to do, babe, fuck?"

"There is but one recourse left to me," Jackson sighed wearily, "in a word, the demon rum. Mayhap there is someone in my immediate vicinity who has a means of locomotion by virtue of which we can joyously abscond to the liquor store to procure for ourselves some peppermint schnapps?"

The waiter came to our table to take further orders, of which there were none.

"A chalice of water, my good man," said Jackson. Upon ascertaining that no ride was available at this table, he took his glass of water and moved on to greener pastures.

Jerry smiled and sipped Alan's coffee. "You know, if we sat here long enough, I'll bet we'd see just about everything in the way

of people . . . I always feel I'll miss something if I don't come."
Almost as if on cue, a young, blond thing sitting at an adjacent
table turned to her escort and squeaked, "I *like* this place; it's a *fun*
place!"

Jerry cringed slightly and laughed, "See what I mean?"

A curious nonentity called Tom "faded" into the shop. He stood
at the door for a moment and looked over the assemblage, then,
singling us out, came over to our table. If I hadn't met him before,
he would be precisely the sort of person I might have expected to
approach us and ask, "Say, I was sitting here an hour ago and I
think maybe I lost my wallet under the table. Do you mind if I
have a look?" Instead, he asked in an apologetic tone, as though
begging an indulgence, "Mind if I join you?" The way he asked it
made one feel that if he had written the request out, he would have
neglected to capitalize the "I."

"Sure, pull up a chair."

The conversation seemed to end suddenly as three pairs of eyes
focused on the newcomer, waiting for him to say something innocuous. "I guess I'll have a cup of coffee," he said finally.

No one seemed to remember Tom's last name. If mentioned
at all, he was designated as *Little* Tom. If someone were to ask,
"Who made the party last night?" the answer might be, "Oh, Dave
and Diane and Lowell and Tom . . ."

"Tom? Tom who?"

"Oh, you know, *Little* Tom," and a hand would be held slightly
above floor level to indicate lack of stature.

Tom was the sort of person perpetually doomed to not having
his last name remembered.

He made the scene for a while (until the day he seemed to fade
into the woodwork and was never seen again), and there was no

reason why he *shouldn't* make the scene . . . any more than there was any reason why he *should*.

He was, as described, a very small man but not so small as to be singularly so (that alone might have saved him from complete nonentity-hood). He wore thick, black-framed glasses that perched on his singularly unremarkable face. His glasses were the only palpable impression that stood out in the memory when, ten minutes after he would leave, someone might vainly try to recall his face.

Perhaps this is the reason why, after he disappeared, we would occasionally talk about him. It is nice to believe that everyone has something singular about him . . . bad breath, a large nose, and abortive disposition. Not Little Tom. His only claim to singularity lay in the fact that he was the most singularly un-singular person imaginable.

He had once announced that he was a painter and had invited Jerry over to see some of his work. Until after his disappearance (when we noticed it . . . a month or so elapsed before someone mentioned that he hadn't been around), Jerry, a fairly competent art critic, had never commented on Little Tom's painting, which was to be expected. He was the sort of person who would paint something that aroused no particular need for comment, pro or con. The only reason his name was ever brought up after he left . . . or his existence acknowledged . . . was because of the conversation that occurred that night in the coffeehouse. He would sit and take in conversation like a sponge, nod knowingly occasionally, and never say much other than "I've found that to be true myself."

As far as could be observed from his conversation, he had done only one thing in his life other than paint. He had read Saint-Exupéry's *The Little Prince*. It was, in his estimation, the finest book ever written, and he would recommend it several times a night to whomever he might be conversing with.

Since conversation was at a lull, Little Tom felt called upon to reactivate it with his views on "this Little Prince." He couldn't quite remember the author's name, though. It was a Freshman . . . Saint something . . . he was sure of that. "That's odd; it slipped my mind."

"Oh yes," said Jerry, with little interest, "Saint Augustine."

"Yes," said Little Tom, "I believe that's correct." He said it with an air of conviction, as though he had known right along that Saint Augustine had written *The Little Prince*.

Jerry caught the cue quickly. His eyes lit up as he launched into an intensely cultural conversation. Alan and I picked up the ball.

"I thought *The Little Prince* was fine, as far as it went," said Jerry, "but I don't think it had the finesse of his later work, *A Journal of the Plague Year*."

"I didn't know he wrote that," Little Tom ventured hesitantly. "Are you positive?"

"No, Jerry," I offered, "you're thinking of Margaret Mitchell."

"Yes, that's right . . . I remember now," Jerry answered.

"That's what I thought," added Little Tom while I went through the incredible pain of trying to keep a straight face.

This was too incredible to believe. We advanced cautiously for a while, until it became obvious that his pride would not allow him to appear ignorant of any of the facts we presented him with in a growing barrage of misinformation. We felt slightly guilty about it but later excused ourselves for the mental dissection on the grounds that proper anesthetic was present in Little Tom's mind.

"That reminds me of Machiavelli's satire on Egyptian metaphysics . . . ," Alan began, and was interrupted by Jerry. "You mean the one Tchaikovsky made into a musical comedy . . . what was it called? . . . *Swallow Lake?*"

"Don't you mean *Swan Lake?*" Little Tom challenged.

"Of course not . . . that's by Stokowski."

"Oh, that's right."

"Yes, there's a fine painting of one of the scenes from it hanging in the Louvre in Rome," added Alan. "Are you familiar with it?"

"I'm not sure. I seem to recall seeing a print of it, but not distinctly."

"Sure, it was painted by Joyce Kilmer, the author of *Leaves of Grass*," I ventured, feeling brave.

"Ah yes," said Alan, "I once saw a self-portrait of Joyce Kilmer. What a fantastically beautiful woman she was. Haunting eyes."

"I'm not familiar with it myself," Little Tom said, "but I've heard about it."

"They say that Van Gogh went mad when he saw it, and that's the reason he cut off his nose," Jerry added.

"I believe it was his ear," Little Tom corrected.

"No . . . that was over a love affair," Jerry defended.

"Of course, I remember now," answered Little Tom, looking mildly confused and uncomfortable. "It must be a powerful painting indeed."

"Indeed," we replied in unison, then gave up all faltering attempts at serious countenance.

We walked back to the room, joking occasionally about Little Tom, kicking up dust left by the heat of the day; dust that left me with a grimy feeling that I could not quite comprehend, because it flew up invisible in the warm night air. I began to attribute the grimy feeling to a growing sense of guilt I felt about so neatly helping to destroy Little Tom. Alan seemed to second-guess my mood and become more sober. "You know, this seems to bother me in a way . . ."

"I know. I catch the same feeling," Jerry added.

"Me too," I said. "I think it boils down to the fact that we suddenly found ourselves in control of Tom's mind . . . able to shape and mold it . . . to actually walk on it. It's sort of a godlike situation, and it showed us a degree of conceit in ourselves to have taken advantage of it."

"A degree of conceit . . . or a manner of conceit, anyway, that's less than desirable," said Alan. "I'm rather ashamed of myself for having it; much less showing it off."

"Oh, bull," Jerry said with slight distaste. "The guy deserved it. Anybody with that much false pride deserves to be knocked down a few notches. The guy's just plain *gross*. Too gross to feel any pain, probably."

"Hey, wait," I answered. "You talk about how well you know people, but that makes me wonder . . ."

"But wait, I mean . . ."

I counter-interrupted, "Anybody who's sensitive enough about his own inadequacies to put up a front like Little Tom does . . . well, it probably hurts him more to be shot down than someone who *does* have something on the ball. The *reason* he does it is because he's sensitive. You know it's a hell of a lot more embarrassing to be caught in a lie than to be caught in the wrong; and that's essentially what he was doing, lying."

"Not to us, though; to himself."

"That's what bothers me, though," said Alan. "What gives us the right to set ourselves up as judges of other men's actions?"

"But what is there that says we can't, by the same token?" Jerry asked.

"Yourself," Alan answered. "We're all a good bit less than perfect ourselves: 'Let he among you who is without sin cast the first stone.'"

"Maybe so," Jerry said.

We walked on in silence for a few minutes, kicking up the invisible dust. "Well," I added as an afterthought, "it was fun." Alan answered with an amused, cocked eyebrow, and Jerry snorted, "Which is criterion enough in many cases, you goddamned moralists."

As we entered the room, Willy moaned. He was lying face down on the huge bed, leisurely stirring a can of water with his fingers. Willy was the "King" of the room, meaning, mainly, that he paid the rent. He stood an even six feet tall, nudging the scale at a hundred and thirty-five pounds. A good deal of his face was rendered invisible by a glorious red beard, and his main interests were love and mysticism.

Willy never said a great deal, or if he did, it was mainly incomprehensible. He smoked many cigarettes and attempted to write books that were, if anything, as incomprehensible as Willy.

"How you doing, Willy?" Jerry asked as we came in.

Willy looked up for a second, then continued to stir his can of water. "Won't tell ya," he muttered.

When asked a question of greater or lesser import, he was prone to answer, "Won't tell ya," but he could, on occasion, wax eloquent on any of the seven lokas, and preferred his lovemaking in the yab-yum position; tying his legs into a bow knot and meditating on the sublime.

His extensive library hung, in a manner threateningly unstable, above his bed, supported by a bowed and rotting timber. It is sometimes said that one can gain great insight into a man by studying his library; this was certainly true of Willy. His selection ranged from such works as *The Rice Economy of Monsoon Asia* or volumes on the imminent threat of flying saucers (where do they come from . . . what are they plotting?!), down to a lonely, untouched volume (half of a set) on aviation electronics and *Metaphysical Meditations on Karma*. In other words, just as it was impossible to make heads or tails out of his reading, it was equally hard to make heads or tails out of Willy. Willy was there. He varied between communism and reactionaryism but could always be found at one extreme pole or the other, politically, mentally, and Willy-wise.

He was an itinerant collector of odds and ends, and one could be sure that if there was a call for something that, under ordinary circumstances, would be of no possible use to anyone, of no conceivable value in any way, shape, or form, Willy had one or two lying about. Be it an empty fruit juice can, a broken television antenna, a box of sanitary napkins, a nondescript piece of heavy metal wire that looked as though it had once been a part of a grander scheme, or one-third of a bottle of castrated female hormones . . . Willy had it. Maybe even two or three. He envisioned an ultimate use for each and every item, and if you happened to throw something away because you were tired of getting up in the middle of the night and tripping over it or were irritated by its continual whir, or were afraid it might bite you when you weren't looking . . . deeming it of no possible consequence whatsoever in the colossal design, Willy would immediately miss it and demand to know its whereabouts.

He was inordinately fond of looming, and I would often wake up in the middle of the night to find Willy looming over me.

When noticed, he would chuckle with satisfaction and go switch the light on and off or set something on fire; since it was Willy, you accepted it and went back to sleep.

As an added attraction to his sideshow, he would, bimonthly or so, compose a prophecy of doom and leave it tacked to the door until such time as he could think of a prophecy for man more devastating than the current, which would then replace the other.

I once sat down at the desk to write a letter and noticed a small, orange card tacked up above the desk that read:

"The Virgin whispered to me in a dream: THE END OF THE WORLD IS COMING EARLY IN FEBRUARY 1962."

Followed by the explanation:

"In the Bible, 'world' is from the Greek AEON, implying civilization, or our structured society."

He would go to elaborate ends to set up a joke and once kept a broken television sitting around for a month. To the question "Does it work?" he would reply, "No, but then, do any of us?"

THERE ARE LONG DAYS AND THERE ARE SHORT DAYS, JUST as there are orange days and gray days (although the calendar does not differentiate them from one another), but always, in between, are the waiting days. They are the days during which time is "observed." Observed time has a tendency to inch slowly, like a worm on a leisurely stroll through the head . . . entering through one ear and, after deciding it has stayed too long already, exiting through the other ear. These are gray days, regardless of the climatic conditions, and they strain the maximum possible monotony from each second . . . wringing it dry after washing it out in water with too much bleach . . . and hanging each minute and hour on a gray wash line, where the sun, if there is any, can steal away whatever color the bleach happened to miss.

The orange days leap by, running hand in hand with the gray days until the latter must stop for wind and then is left behind. Gray days leave you with various soft, doughy lumps in your body and mind and a vague feeling that you should take a bath until you realize that the grime and the grease are intangible, soluble only in the brilliant bath of an orange day. The reason a day is gray is because you haven't shaved . . . or you slept so late that the day is fading . . . or you itch in a place that is inaccessible and you don't have the energy to scratch anyway, so you continue to itch, realizing dully that it is impossible to scratch your brain.

Sometimes the gray will filter in on an orange day; not too much, but just enough to indicate its presence, and suddenly, you feel content. Not depressed; not exuberant . . . just content. The trouble with contentment is that it is addictive and harder to shake than junk. You find yourself sitting at a window observing a not-too-beautiful-but-not-really-bad-either day and not paying a hell of a lot of attention to it, because, after all, it *is* there, and it's nice, and what else is there to say? And when you suddenly catch yourself thinking in terms of "nice" rather than fantastic or great, or terrible and disgusting, and when all of a sudden you realize that you've been thinking that way since you can remember . . . suddenly, your back bends a little and you begin to notice gray hairs. If, then, you continue being content, or not caring a lot, you may consider yourself a member of the legion of the addicted . . . and you feel slightly sad about that; not depressed or fearful . . . just sad, and that, too, is a form of content. Perhaps you may consider writing a book about the days when you were *not* content, and it seems a "nice" idea, even as you sit at the window and watch the autumn wind carry a few drab leaves away; leaves that will never again glow with the green of spring, but mulch the ground, beneath a snowy shroud, to ensure the coming greenness of the dormant grass. And then the snow comes, but you may not see it because you've turned away to sip your drink or rearrange the few books in your bookshelf because they've been shuffled about by some careless hand probably concerned with neither the various volumes nor their contents; possibly your own.

There is waiting; waiting for you know not what . . . never certain that it will come, but waiting against the day when it might. And the thought that it could come at any moment, even when you're not around to meet it with drum and cannon . . . in which case you might never know it had come and gone in your absence, perhaps not to return . . . assumes command of your once free leash and the soles on your shoes last a year instead of four weeks as they used to. But you are content to wait with faith in whatever it is that is to come, and to be comfortable. Those who observe you, though they don't think twice about it nor think to tell you . . . know that "it" *has* come . . . and "its" name is "Nice."

It was on "waiting" days that Jerry would be struck with the desire to go to the coffee shop because "I have a feeling that something is going to happen, and I don't want to miss it." The coffee shop manager became increasingly belligerent as we graced potentially paying tables with our unwashed selves, spending the entire evening over a single cup of coffee (not apiece but for all of us) night after night. He usually spoke to Jerry, who, by virtue of being the prime target, became more and more verbally expressive when told: "Look, Jerry, you're making me tell you once too often now; you and your buddies are ruining my business. You all sit here and don't buy anything . . . that alone costs me more than you're all worth . . . but you not only scare away potential customers, you *drive away* any that have been paying."

"But look at it this way," Jerry might answer, "it's your *business*, but it's *our home*. You're rendering a great service to the community besides; you keep us off the streets at night . . ."

And Alan would add, "Besides, sir, the colossal scheme of things seems to dictate that we sit here, which, in due course, we do. You stand in danger of jeopardizing the whole structure of destiny by your rash proclamations."

After several disgruntled comments and the reluctant purchase of a few more cups of coffee, he would be temporarily appeased, returning to the back of the store to redden his nose and fortify his faltering courage with a quick snort from his oft-discussed jug. He remained appeasable until the night when a score or more of the group, after a Friday-night party, converged on his establishment at once rather than insidiously and quietly filtering in (the method by which we previously, and wisely, fortified our front). We filed in, a mounting flow filling the aisle. The manager's eyes flashed fire as I, the somewhat uncertain Moses heading the line (because I had a fairly decent sport coat on and pretty Barbara to hang on my arm and look bewildered and innocent at whatever he might insinuate), came up against his hands-on-hips blockade.

"Just keep walking," he breathed, defending his few empty tables, which waited patiently for Friday-night dinner patrons. He manually about-faced me, unassailably directing a countermarch back to the door. And that was an end to it; thereafter, he met us at the door. Alan, only would he admit, being impressed with the Englishman's faultless manner and meticulous dress, continuously wondering aloud as to why Alan should choose to associate himself with such displeasing compatriots.

The rousing "Two, four, six, eight, we won't integrate" untactfully led by Willy's rabble-rousing girlfriend [unclear] did little to better further relations as we filed out, so we were left coffeehouseless.

The local bookstore, previously populated only sparsely, became the focal point of operations. A section in the back of the store was furnished with tables and chairs. I walked to the bookstore every day and sat there, afraid to miss whatever-it-was for which I was waiting; always with the half-formed feeling that whatever-it-was left just before I came or would come not too long after I had to leave. I waited, though, with the unexamined conviction that someday "it" and I would miraculously be there at the same time. Sometimes I would hear a click of heels or see a flash of bright clothing from the corner of my eye, and I would feel like jumping up to see if this was what I had been waiting for.

There were parties, many of them, and each of us devoutly made the scene; each time with the vague, unspoken feeling that this would be the one where "it" would appear, and, of course, it wouldn't, so we would drink whatever was around and have a good time and watch the door in case "it" came in. And when, invariably, "it" didn't appear, we would vow not to waste any more time partying, but we did, anyway, because we were sure afraid that it might be there and we wouldn't.

If, perchance, a party was missed, later reports would seem to indicate that that was the *one* party, of all the scores of parties, that should never have been missed.

Fingers became stained with nicotine, but whatever it was that one smoked for wasn't to be found, it seemed; at least not *this* time . . . but maybe in the next one. (The phrase "They Satisfy" pertaining to a cigarette seemed suddenly to become self-damning, as well as obviously absurd, because once satisfied, you would never need to smoke again. And perhaps then "it" would have arrived.)

While we were waiting, we learned one another, for this was a time when all guards were down and pretention was ridiculous on its face, except in jest. Guards were down, but never the faith of the true believer . . . at least not in the conviction that "it" would one day walk through that very door.

Jerry once confided to me that "the fear of not being here when what I'm waiting for walks in undermines my very existence." It was then I began to realize that the far-reaching roots of the diseased plant of centuries, the twisting, grasping roots that burrow into the mind and decay the body . . . the vines that root man to the soil beneath the shade of a comforting tree (or, perhaps, in the wicked, withering heat of the day) . . . that bind his limbs to those of the plow with ethereal, yet unbreakable, tendrils, busying him eternally across the sunbaked earth sowing the secure seed that promises he shall not go without bread (nor shall the owner of the land upon which he crops, and though it be a whiter, richer bread upon which he dines, it is such that it satisfies no more than the crude loaf seasoned with sweat); the roots that hold the head to the ground, twisted into an invisible noose, viewing only the soil that is always there, unlike the stars, which disappear in daylight and change with the seasons; it was then that I began to realize that these were the roots that had spread through *my* body and attempted to hold me fast to a puddle stagnating with the weeds and disease from which it nourished its vines.

Jerry . . . who had quit school at sixteen to ride the rails and seek his fortune . . . who, a precocious artist with a gifted brush had set aside the paint and canvas to dedicate himself, against a strong chorus of "You're wasting a God-given talent," to digging folk songs out of dusty archives and mutilated, old 78 records . . . and if his voice was not of Caruso timbre, so much the better; "Makes it more ethnic" was his defense, and he had records to prove it . . . It was a considerably more "respectable" Jerry who, after many months and many "scenes," said: "You know, Bob, sometimes I get the feeling that whatever we were waiting for came and left, and we never knew it, even though it stayed for quite a while. I guess it didn't wear a sign around its neck like we thought it would, so we couldn't accept it."

"I don't quite get you," I answered.

"Think about it for a minute."

When I thought back (how much stronger hindsight is than foresight) upon the "scene" that had absorbed my waking and dreaming hours for the best part of a year, all I could do was shrug as the loose strands braided into a single cord in my mind . . . a cord that ran consistent through the spring "waiting" and through the days of summer and into the fall . . . the winter when it snowed for the first time in thirty-five years around these parts (and a good half foot or more in places, at that). Only when "it" had gone were we given the magical spectacles with which to see; the spectacles that maturity cannot do without, just as youth cannot comprehend the need for. Only then did it become apparent that "it" had been there all along: joining our conversations, walking with us on early mornings when we combed the streets for cigarette butts, singing with us, and philosophizing with us . . . and even waiting with us.

It was primarily while sitting in the bookstore waiting that we developed and expounded our individual philosophies. The brunt of much of our theorizing was that most ambivalent of concepts: security.

"CAN YOU IMAGINE ANYTHING MORE COMFORTABLY INNOCUOUS than a man going through life with a forty-pound security on his back?" Jerry asked during the course of a particularly long and unexciting afternoon, casting about for conversation to ease, or at least camouflage, the monotony.

I thought it over and replied with what I calculated would wrap the conversation up and allow me to continue stewing in my not-really-unpleasant stagnation processes: "Nothing except maybe a man going through life *looking* for a forty-pound security to strap on. That more or less catches anyone I've ever met. One or the other, I mean."

He looked worried for a moment. "You might be right . . . maybe that's what *we're* doing sitting around here . . . a big, fat security, man, maybe that's what we're waiting for, expecting him to come in the front door with a basket of hamburgers in one hand and a pack of unsmoked butts in the other. I'd be inclined to quit if I was sure of that."

"Quit what?"

"Ha! There's the rub. Quit breathing, maybe, but I don't think it has to be as drastic as that."

"We're safe, in any case. Such things don't seem to have a habit of walking in doors and saying, 'Give me your tired, your poor . . . here I is!'"

"Maybe that's why we're still waiting." He picked up his guitar and ran a fingernail down the bass string, producing a grating squeak.

"Maybe . . ."

Alan came in, bearing a rosebud in his fingers. The rosebud was his daily gift to the bookstore, and people would glance oddly at him as he swept in holding the frail blossom tenderly, depositing it in a cola bottle full of water, oblivious to the wondering looks.

Ceremony completed, he sat down at our table. "Oreos make you fat," he announced.

"Sounds like a good subject for your thesis."

"It's already been written, you know. Some bloody lady poet in New York." Alan was fond of punctuating his sentences with gracious sweeps of the hand. The cola bottle with the rosebud hit the deck.

"Oh dear, how embarrassing," he said, and immediately began to dab here and there with his handkerchief. Jerry raised an eyebrow that seemed as if to say, "I've said it before, so why bother," and began to pick out blues on his guitar.

After sweeping up his debris and returning the broom, Alan sat down and thumbed through his notebook. "I've written an immortal poem," he said.

"Immoral, eh?" Jerry answered.

"Please, more sobriety, if you will. I spent the afternoon trying to decide upon a title for it. 'The Primordial Writhing Was the Void' caught my fancy for a while but sounds a little pretentious, I suppose."

"Well, what did you come up with?"

"After due consideration, I've decided to title it 'Poem.'"

"Wild."

I sometimes like to sleep in logs,
Or crawl in bogs,
Or howl at dogs;
Howl Jowel.
They say my nose is red,
As is my bed
And toolshed. Howl Jowel,
Hell fell into the dell.

"I, too, am a poet of sorts," said Jerry, "and there's one little verse that's been running through my mind for quite a while now. I'm sure you'd all like to see it." He took Alan's notebook and scribbled down a verse in his illegible handwriting. Alan looked at it for a moment. "I'm dreadfully sorry, but I'm afraid I've let slip on my archaeology. I really can't make heads or tails out of hieroglyphics anymore." He passed it on to me.

"They say bad handwriting is a mark of genius. If this is true, I need not even look at the poem to realize it is a work of art," I added, and passed it back to Jerry, who cleared his throat and read:

Carmudgeon, curbludgeon,
Kergwimble, kerblank,
I'm gonna rob
The First National Bank.

"What essential beauty; what depth of soul," I commented.

"Perhaps," added Alan, "but a shade too sentimental in stylistic construct."

"I don't claim to understand you modern romanticists," I said, looking through my own notebook, which I generally carried either for effect or just in case I should be hit by a flash of inspiration . . . or to write down snatches of conversation that I could later plagiarize at leisure for my own devices.

"You're insane, Father William," the young man said,
"And your bowels have become very tight,
And yet you incessantly quote Karl Marx,
Do you think, at your age, this is bright?"

"In my youth," said the old man, most vehemently,
"I feared it would cost me my head,
But now that I find no one else has one,
Why, I've joined the Elks Club instead."

"It appears to me that nothing short of a cultural renaissance is being formed in the womb of this humble bookstore," Alan exclaimed.

"Damned right," Jerry said. "They might not know they've been existing in a dark age, but we'll show 'em."

"Right," I said. "We'll teach them that waiting for the Security Man can be a real art."

Jerry picked at his guitar for a moment, then said, "Well, now that you've 'bum-kicked' everyone, would you care to expound?"

"Might as well. It'll help to bide time until he gets here."

"Lay on, Macduff." He started to play the guitar louder and louder. "Maybe I can drown you out and preserve my virginity."

"You're both out of your minds," Alan concluded.

"Or maybe too far in them," I added, perversely relishing the double-edged sword I was momentarily wielding.

ALL OVER THE WORLD, THE INSECT OF SOCIAL IRRITATION WAS making known his presence. We were as much a product of the times as of anything else: a time devoid of new physical horizons and a time that was forced to seek within for the conflicts nature could no longer afford us. The well-explored, carefully charted world that had been offered to us at birth was discarded, with its figurehead kings and be-highwayed jungles, as devoid of either interest or worth. Even so, we had a faith in ourselves similar to the proverbial flea crawling up an elephant's leg with rape on its minds, as we freed ourselves from the world of manners and polite society that we might reenter it on our own terms, if at all. The rejection necessarily included loss of its comforts, and coffee, the staff of life, assumed the position of its richer brother, the cocktail.

And always, we waited. We questioned the waiting but were powerless against it. We waited without knowing for what we waited or why, but we waited with a vengeance and talked about many things. We talked about the college that taught us to dig Keats and then offered us a degree in insurance salesmanship. We talked about social security, the shining goal that loomed half a century away and demanded only our lives in payment. It was us, above all, who realized our consecrated goal, for we knew that Peter Pan would die if no one believed in fairies, and so we believed in fairies (and their equivalents) because it was very important that Peter Pan not die.

We were not a majority, so we could do little when Uncle Sam tapped us. We went through basic training in a sort of hypnotic trance as we were taught to execute the things we preferred to pretend did not exist while the sergeant in charge of bayonet training asked us through his battery-powered loudspeaker, "What is the spirit of the bayonet, men?" We would answer as we have through the years, in unison, as we had been taught, "To kill," then he would say, "Let's hear a little more spirit," as though he were a high school cheerleader, except that he wanted to hear "Kill" instead of "Hold that line," and we would holler louder, "To kill!"

"I still can't hear anything. If you men want a smoke break, I'd better be able to hear you this time . . . now, WHAT IS THE SPIRIT OF THE BAYONET?"

"TO KILL!" And that was better, so we got our smoke break. Even then, we waited, but we had something positive *to* wait for then: for our hitches to end, only to find out that the only difference between army life and civilian life was that the army life was more honest. At least they told you that you were nothing more than a machine to them (not the officers, of course . . . they learned about morale and such in OCS, but the old sergeants knew the score and let you know it too). Back in civilian life, they played Lawrence Welk music on the production lines and tried, with varying degrees of success, to give you the impression that Horsdung Enterprises Inc. was Daddy, security blanket, and God; an air-conditioned, employer-employee relationshipped, wage-scaled holy trinity with 5 percent of your yearly earnings in the form of a Christmas Bonus masquerading as the Virgin Mary.

It is sad to be disillusioned, but I wasn't sad; therefore I suppose that title didn't fit. Disillusionment comes when you become absolutely sure that "it" will *never* walk through that door you've been watching at for so long . . . or any other door. So I waited and occasionally broke a fingernail or swatted languidly at a fly and watched people come in who weren't really people, but, then, who weren't really *not* people either.

"Hey, Jerry, dig that old guy."

"Wow, he looks like he's been through the mill a couple of times."

"A leftover from the Charge of the Light Brigade, huh?"

The old guy looked for all the world like what a "people" must be. It was written all over his face in lines half an inch deep, the whole bit: suffering, love, hate . . . and here he was, not five yards from us; the ultimate human being. He began to browse through the magazine section, looked both ways to ascertain (wrongly) that he was not being watched, then furtively picked up a copy of *Sunbathing* and dug the nudists. Then, just in case he *was* being watched, he shook his head disapprovingly, put the magazine down, and picked up *Mechanix Illustrated*. His interest in the magazine became quite intense as a priest brushed by him and excused himself. He waited a good thirty seconds to make sure the priest was out of sight, then slyly picked up *Sunbathing* again, dug the nudists for a few more furtive seconds, shook his head in disapproval again, then put it down.

"You know," I said to Jerry, "I think I've seen almost every type of person imaginable digging the nudists. Every one of them feels an obligation to shake his head at the shame and put it down again. I'm beginning to feel sorry for the nudists. Doesn't anybody approve?"

"No one seems to, but their magazines generally sell out the first day or two after they get on the rack. I never see anybody buy them, though. The whole thing's pretty damned mysterious."

"Oh, there's a method for buying them, you know. You also have to buy a cultural book, *Studies in Etymology* or something by Sartre, for example. This proves to whoever happens to see you slink to the counter with it that you're really a person of culture and have a well-rounded interest in the many facets of life. Not that you approve . . ."

PERHAPS ONE OF THE THINGS I WAS WAITING FOR IN THOSE DAYS was to see someone pick that goddamned magazine up, sit down at a table in full view of priests, grandmothers, et cetera, allow his tongue to extend lewdly to his chin, and just dig the holy hell out of the nudists.

This might start a minor revolution of sorts. There is something so convincing about a man who innocently and straightforwardly does what he damned well *wants* to do (when it is within the bounds of reason) that others naturally follow him. In the meantime, the bulk of humanity huddles together at an intersection with no cars in sight, waiting for the light to change to green so that they can cross the street (the green light perhaps indicating that the invisible death ray has been turned away from the intersection until the next red light). Suddenly, out of nowhere, appears a leader of the people; liberator of the common man. He sees no cars and, therefore, quite naturally begins to cross the street, red light, death ray, and all. The crowd watches him in awe, hesitates for a moment, teetering on the colossal curb, then begins to cross the forbidden street looking somewhat nervous, as a group, but reminiscently Errol Flynn–ish nonetheless. One or two might wonder why they hesitated in the first place, unwilling to accept the fact that they had awaited just such a leader, not realizing that they had taken part in a revolution as unmistakable as any that ever happened in France or Cuba.

Meanwhile, we waited. And every second that we waited, a new automobile rolled from a showroom window and fishtailed onto the highways; a new entity was ushered, protestingly, from warm nothingness into life to begin *its* wait, and television slowly but surely vanquished *The Wizard of Oz*.

ABOUT 75 PERCENT OF THE JOURNEY FROM THE ROOM TO the bookstore was without the aid of sidewalks, and I doubt if grass has yet grown over the well-trodden path I made. Sometimes the trek was made for company, sometimes with the not-too-brilliant hope of running into someone who would be overcome to generosity by the loud, incessant growl of my nearly always empty stomach. I occasionally entertained myself as I walked, humming a two-part fugue with my grumbling stomach sounding a steady rising and falling bass note, only to sit in the store for a while as the growls of my compatriots added several additional parts to the impromptu invention. I would sit until the sitting became intolerable and then walk back, frustrated, wondering why I had gone in the first place; knowing that I would go again, many times, before this peculiar stage of my existence came to a slow, uncertain halt.

At one end of the path, the bookstore end, lay romance, excitement, adventure (potentially), and waiting (almost invariably). At the other end, the room end, the Blind Prophet and resignation. Resignation . . . but only temporarily, of course. Until the next time the inevitable, intangible, latent prodding again set my undernourished mechanism upon a four-mile path to Mecca. And, each time, Mecca moved a little further into the ethereal. Like an animal it moved . . . grazing contentedly in lush pastures until it catches the scent of the hunter, then scurrying to a farther pasture, a more inaccessible ground. Perhaps the hunter catches a glimpse of his quarry, but it is too late, for the beast is gone, leaving him to ponder whether or not the hunt is worth the effort. With dusk rapidly coming on, he decides to break open his breech and head for home. And so the game continues until, quite suddenly, hunting season is over . . . and as he leaves the forest to begin his journey home, he may spot the animal grazing, unaware, on the grass that surrounds his camp. But it is too late; his gun is broken down and oiled, and the season has ended. He may smile, in his impotence, or clench his fist into a hard, frustrated ball . . . but, no matter, take it as he will, the season has gone the way of seasons before, and winter is pushing on.

THE MORE OFTEN ONE WALKS A FAMILIAR PATH, THE SHORTER IT seems to become. But this is a mental attitude, and muscles still become tired, especially muscles depending on a rarely used stomach for nourishment. My shoes were muddy, and my mind felt the same way. I kicked them off as I entered the room, finding, to add another irritant to the heap, that my socks were in the same condition (by virtue of well-worn soles). "Damnation," I muttered as I peeled them off and put them on the heater to dry. It was the kind of day when minor irritations come from all sides, bouncing lightly off a growing shell of apathy . . . each asking only a half-hearted "damn" before they scurry off to join their fellows. I lay down on the monstrous bed with the notion of sleeping through the rest of the dreary day and awakening to a world of sunshine and daffodils.

A sudden thought crossed my mind as I felt a small reserve of strength succumb to drowsiness. People die all the time; sometimes for no apparent reasons. Maybe this would be *my* time. The thought didn't really displease me. Maybe I'd lived a complete life . . . damned dull, if true . . . but, nevertheless, conceivably complete. The more I thought about it, the surer I became that such was the case, even though aware that I was half-asleep. An intellectual curiosity overcame me. Here I was dying, and it didn't bother me very much. Strange thought . . . I could feel my limbs becoming light and pliable as my muscles began to lose control of them.

I wished idly for a cup of coffee and a cigarette but decided that I didn't really want either. A car horn honked, and I became aware of traffic sounds on the nearby rain-soaked highway. The sounds seemed to come from another world . . . an incredibly, comfortably, distant world of which I was not a part. I looked out the window at a dull, cloudy sky before my eyes closed. That was peaceful. Dreary days are nice in a way. They give one a sense of perspective; give a ceiling to infinity instead of stretching eternally upward into the black that lies beyond the blue of the sky. I heard the patter of rain tattooing lightly against the window, and that was good too. There are few feelings so sweet and secure as that of drifting through a liquid void while the rain beats futile against your protective shell. The rain's monotonous pitter-pat began to fade, and I knew that I would soon be dead. It was pleasant . . . I'd never thought it would be pleasant, but it was . . . very pleasant . . . drifting about, bodiless; drifting toward a nonexistent cavern of nothingness. A nothingness as perpetual as one always believes life to be until one is dying . . . and warm. Very warm . . . drifting, with only the rain, very soft, touching, tapping, fading . . . and the void, all-encompassing, warm . . . like something out of the past; the past where memory cannot define, only remember; as life began, so it ends . . . drifting upon a soft, unfelt ocean . . .

Then, even the sound of rain was gone, but I was still aware. I didn't want to be aware, but I was. It was disappointing; disappointing not to be nothing and to become one with the sweet, warm drift. My eyes were not open, but I could sense the shimmering green all about me. There was a pulsation, and the pulsation was the shimmer, and the shimmer was green . . . green glass. The glass curved on all sides of me, arching above my head and extending into the distance. I guessed it to be a hallway of some sort. I started to move down the hall and heard a sharp click ring through the cavernous depths as my heels touched the polished black obsidian of the floor. I couldn't feel my body, and the sounds caused by my movement seemed independent of my motion. I seemed to be "willing" my way forward rather than walking. The sensation was strange and unfamiliar.

I seemed to be moving forward for a long time, but I had no idea *how* long, for the idea of time seemed suddenly without meaning. I was moving through a static plane wherein minutes, hours, and centuries had no base from which to spring; no timepiece upon which to be calculated.

I continued to move, becoming vaguely aware that a presence other than my own was in the hall. It was no tangible presence, but I could feel it around me and within me, observing my motions and willing me to continue moving.

I stopped.

Who's there? I thought, not being able to vocalize, and the echo of my thought reverberated against the walls; the luminescence becoming brighter and brighter, although my eyes were not involved in the perception.

Suddenly, an abrupt silence as the echo of my voice was absorbed into the shimmering green like a stray droplet of rain falling onto a sponge. A voice entered my mind. The sound was hollow and ringing as though spoken at the mouth of a quiet tunnel.

The voice did not speak in words, but its sound conveyed the intended images into my mind. I felt a sudden anger. Why was the voice interrupting my state of death . . . why was I in this hall or even conscious? I began to feel that I was entangled in some sort of perverse scheme that would allow me no peace, even in death.

At the end of the hall, I sensed a massive door. As the voice rang through my mind, I was made aware that beyond the door lay the ultimate culmination of life.

A tight hand seemed to grip my mind at the realization. The voice told me that I could go or not go through the door as I desired. I felt relieved for a moment. The voice became silent. A deathly still pervaded the hall as I stared at the door and wondered.

There was no appeal to mercy, obviously . . . for no judgment had been levied; I could go or not go as I pleased, but once I had opened the door, I understood, I was obligated to enter.

The presence disappeared entirely, but I took no notice as I stood before the door wondering. There was no hurry, I had been advised. The door would always be there, waiting to be opened . . . waiting to unveil its secret or not, as I chose; whatever I chose . . .

Suddenly, the full weight of realization flooded over me, and I prayed for unconsciousness while the reverberations of my prayers dashed against the walls of glass and seemed to shatter my mind into a million fragments that immediately reassembled themselves to be shattered anew.

The door stood innocently in front of me, waiting to be opened, and I wondered if I ever would.

I sat down on the floor, facing the door, to wait . . . not knowing what else to do, and the sound I made rang across the expanse of the hall and tore back into my mind.

I SEEMED TO BE SPIRALING UP FROM A GREAT DEPTH AS I RETURNED to consciousness. A vague fog met my eyes as they opened, through which pierced rays of brilliantly pigmented colors. I suddenly became aware of a face staring down at me as from a great height. As my mind cleared, the features of the face consolidated into Willy, who was engaged in his favorite pastime: looming over sleeping people. The colors resolved themselves into the Christmas tree lights that he had haphazardly strung across the room.

"What in hell are you doing, Willy?" I asked, massaging my arm, which had gone to sleep. I knew damned well that he was doing nothing except being Willy (which is exception enough in itself).

"Won't tell ya," he answered, and cackled mysteriously, lighting the end of his beard on fire, then snuffing it out. He continued being Willy, dancing around the room, setting things on fire.

I lay on the mattress and watched him, asking myself, "What is an apparently normal person like you doing associating with such complete nuts?" and answered, "What makes you think you're so damned normal?" "I guess it's all a matter of degree . . . proper perspective and relatively, you know." "Could be."

"Anything happening tonight, Willy?"

He paused for a minute, then sat down and assumed the lotus position to meditate. He sat there for some time, his legs interlaced under him, and appeared to be in profound consternation. His eyes suddenly brightened as the answer occurred to him. He crossed and uncrossed his eyes several times and then said, "What's it to ya?"

"Come off it. I just asked what's happening?"

"Ha, I thought so. Won't tell ya."

"For Christ's sake, must you always be so damned difficult?" I asked, becoming irritated.

"Difficult . . . ," he muttered, reassuming the meditative posture. He sat there for some time, then looked up, again enlightened. "Difficult. D-i-f-f-i-c-u-l-t. *D* as in *diphthong*, *I* as in *ichthyology*, *F* as in *flagellation* and again as in *fornication*, *I* as in *infantile paralysis*, *C* as in *communist*, *U* as in *Ukrainian Soviet Socialist Republic*, *L* as in *lacerations of the head and kidneys*, *T* as in *Chinese religion*."

"Chinese religion?"

"*Taoism*, obviously."

"Oh; and what is this all supposed to be indicative of, other than an obvious crying need for psychiatric assistance?"

"You'll find it in Zachariah 2:6; 'Ho ho, saith the Lord.'"

I was never fully convinced that Willy was quite as much a nut as he seemed. It was possible that he just enjoyed doing off-the-wall things, and in his understood status as raving lunatic, he knew that people would overlook them.

If anyone else were to throw open the front door at four o'clock in the morning screaming, "Yngve is a louse!" (a phrase from a fantasy novel that had tickled his fancy), waking half a dozen people from happy slumber, then chuckling gleefully, people might begin to wonder. People didn't wonder about Willy; it was more or less expected of him.

Willy thoroughly enjoyed his status as nut. He seemed born to loom over sleeping people and to write incomprehensible literature.

He sat down at the desk and begin to write something or other, and I felt myself beginning to drift back to sleep. I hovered over the verge of slumber for a few seconds but began to feel uneasy. I opened one eye slowly. Willy was looming over me with a toothy grin.

"Hell." I got up and brushed away the cobwebs of sleep. I shrugged mentally and reached for my socks. There was no use in pursuing the matter. A man's home (or room) is his castle, and this was Willy's castle. He was perfectly within his rights to be just as mad as he wished within its confines. I slipped on my shoes and left the room, more or less following whatever direction my feet cared to prescribe.

The rain had slowed to a drizzle, and a full moon was trying somewhat vainly to squeeze through low-hanging clouds.

I wondered what Willy did when no one was around to react to his madness. He was a great guy, God knew. In spite of his idio-syncrasies, if Willy had a bed, everyone had a bed; if Willy had cigarettes, everyone had cigarettes . . . maybe even more of them than Willy took. Willy was the kind of person who somehow made you wonder just who *you* were, where you were going, and if maybe he didn't have the right idea after all. Good old Willy . . . who six months later was to shave off his magnificent beard sym-bolizing a congealed love affair (an affair, the end of which showed everyone, to their surprise, that Willy could hate quite as vehe-mently as he could love), put on a wrinkled white shirt with a ring of dirt around the collar, and ask himself where he intended to go in such elaborate finery, then stand still for half an hour and say, "Oh God," over and over because somewhere in a mind of undoubted genius a circuit was not making contact, and eventually go to work as a full-time babysitter (nine hours a day, but that was all right because it was a lovely little girl who sometimes called him "Daddy") and collect forty dollars a month for the work while he wrote an incomprehensible book that, in the four pages he eventually completed, after working out one hundred and eighty carefully planned pages of incomprehensible outline, was so sad with the beauty of hopelessness that no editor would look past the first page . . . and his occasional talk of "Jazz America," where all the factories were underground and the outer world was a forest where man could be the unicorn he had always wanted to be, under the shade of the crescent-fruited marijuana tree . . . who sacrificed a faint resemblance to Charlton Heston because a crew cut was more comfortable and he needn't bother with combing it, and it didn't matter anyhow, because beauty of soul was the criterion for judgment in Jazz America.

My wandering had carried me in the direction of Marty's place, so I decided what the hell, I'd drop in and see what was up with the jovial misanthrope.

Marty seemed to have set up an obstacle course, as first I tripped over his motor scooter in the dark driveway, then the top step of his unlighted porch, and shocked myself soundly on his out-of-order-please-knock doorbell.

A face appeared at the window and glared out suspiciously before the door opened. "Well, Bob. Come on in. It's good to see you."

"You mean it's lucky to see me," I answered, commenting on his obstacle course.

"And to what," he asked, ushering me, "do I owe this unheralded visit?" Marty was quite convinced, for no apparent reason, that he was universally despised and so suspected ulterior motivation behind even something so innocent as a visit from an acquaintance.

"Oh, no reason really. Just a chance whim of fate. I started out with nowhere particular in mind, and here I am."

"Nowhere?" he asked as though slighted.

"Well, hi, Grace," I said, peering across the darkened room at a figure in the hide-a-bed sofa, ignoring the question entirely. "What are you doing here?"

"And why *shouldn't* she be here?" Marty demanded, becoming almost insistent on being insulted, if only tokenly.

"Oh, good God . . . ," I muttered under my breath.

"I have some coffee on the stove," Marty added. "I suppose you want some."

"Don't trouble yourself, old bean. You need it more than I do, what with the price of coffee."

"Oh, that's all right. Third time through the grounds anyway."

"Well, all right, in that case." He went into the kitchen to draw a cup for me. There was nothing like a visit to Marty's to make you feel like you shouldn't visit Marty's very often.

"Cream?" he hollered from the kitchen.

"Sure." He brought a jar of home-mixed skim milk back to the living room. Grace Marie winked at me, and I smiled.

Marty caught the exchange. "What's that all about?" he demanded suspiciously.

"Private joke," Grace Marie answered, and began to pare her fingernails.

Marty was a "retired" English teacher at age twenty-six; retired because of his "progressive" attitude. He was quite bitter about the whole matter and spent no end of time brooding and expounding over the subject. He was a man whose holy mission in life seemed to be the acquisition of as many wrongs as possible. He even went so far as to write a volume of poems about how screwed up everything and everyone was; paid a hundred dollars in advance to have it printed up by a friend with access to a duplicating machine . . . and was cemented irretrievably in his convictions when the erstwhile printer made the scene with Marty's hundred and lost the lovingly typed stencils in transit.

Grace Marie sat silently and watched Marty as he tore up hunks of a cardboard box that had housed the parts of a do-it-yourself amplifier kit he had bought, throwing body and soul into its construction for three days. He had later taken the completed mechanism back to the radio store so that they could make it work. He threw the pieces of cardboard into the fireplace and touched a match to them. The fire caught, and he returned to the sofa. As the flames caught and grew, he settled his massive frame into the cushions and attempted to look content (as one should, of course, in front of a fire).

Watching him, in the silence, a distortion of Milton crossed my mind: "Marty's in his element; all's wrong with the world."

The fire had a dull, ferocious roar that lasted for only a few minutes while the sheets of cardboard expended themselves into varied flickering tongues of flame that changed shapes instantaneously as I watched them; no shape enduring so long that it was not immediately replaced by another before its particular, never to be repeated, exactness of form vanished with the smoke that

hurtled up the vacuum of the chimney to dissipate in the vast-
ness of the night sky . . . perhaps to drift leisurely over the town,
mingling with currents of air that might carry it across the sea to
fulfill obligations elsewhere. And perhaps it might merge with the
London fog then or descend in a gentle vapor of rain to quench a
distant fire.

Marty reached up and turned off the dim lamp, and the room
was no less bright for its lack. His cat sat in front of the fire until
the heat became too intense; the "classic" cat, observing the birth
of a flame, sitting upright with its tail curled around its body
until the truth of the heat threatened to singe its whiskers. Then it
moved away and lay down to knit at the rug, watching intently lest
the flames try to escape from their brick boudoir.

"Say, what happened to that gal you were with last night . . .
what's her name, Ann?" Marty asked me as he turned the light
back on.

"Oh, I sent her home. I was getting tired of feminine
irrationality."

Grace Marie looked up, amused by my half-conscious conceit.
"How intolerant of you, oh Golden One."

"Oh, hell . . . I don't include you in that category. You don't
count. It was just your bad luck to be born a woman."

"I don't regret it." Grace Marie grinned toothsomely. She had
the intelligence and perception to be quite wicked, but got a great
deal of pleasure out of playing at bewildered femininity. She rather
fancied the intricacies of being a woman. She also got no end of
enjoyment in needling me with such stocks as "When you can
meet me on my own ground, you'll be a man." However, she
refused to be met on her own ground. She would hit me with what
she considered to be a telling squelch and would then refuse (quite

68

refuse) to be bested, no matter how ornate my return. It would be difficult to ascertain who was more amused by whom.

"Oh, Marty . . . where's that book you wanted me to borrow?"

"I don't know . . . on the shelf probably."

"What's it about?" I asked half interestedly.

Marty leaned back on the couch and thought for a minute. He liked to choose his words carefully, finding the proper word for each slot in a sentence, all of which resulted in concise, if not ponderous, speech.

"Well . . ." He settled back and stared glazedly at the embers of his fire. "It's about a poet who is struggling helplessly against a background of modern inquisitions and intolerance, which sets itself up as a court to judge beauty in terms of how closely it parallels *Dick and Jane*. He's up against a jury of phony prophets with preconceived ideas of what beauty should be . . . people who pretend to abhor commercial art and television poetry and then write the same tripe in book form in order to make the bestseller list . . ."

"Sounds realistic enough," I ventured. "I've never yet met a poet who didn't give the impression that he believed himself to be the sole possessor of a sense of true beauty. Poets have a basic intolerance for anyone who thinks differently than they do and still sounds off about having a sense of beauty."

"Well, that's a little off the—" Marty began.

"Hell," Grace Marie interrupted, "that doesn't go for poets alone. It's the same in any station in life . . . The bourgeoisie have the same kind of intolerance for the rest of the middle class. They each carry on about how they're really different from the rest of their run-of-the-mill class. 'I may work from eight to five, but boy do I swing in the evenings . . .'"

"Here now, we've discovered a universal concept!" I exclaimed.

Grace Marie looked at me over the tops of her glasses, thought for a minute, picked up an emery board, and began to pare her nails. "Eat it," she answered, indicating that she was finished with the conversation.

NO ONE KNEW QUITE WHAT TO MAKE OF JOHN FOR SEV-
eral weeks after he "dropped around" to peruse the scene.
"Now, man, I've been around," he had said as an overture, "and I've seen scenes and I've seen scenes. Some of
them last, and some of them die off before anybody really notices
they're around. The ones that stay are the ones that have *organization*, and that's what this scene needs . . . organization."

I looked up from a magazine and nodded, then continued to
read. Jerry looked up from the same magazine, which he had been
reading over my shoulder—breathing asthmatically—nodded,
and continued to read.

"Who is that guy?" he asked later. "Some kind of nut?"

"Damned if I know . . . He's been hanging around the bookstore for a couple of days. First time he came in, he asked me what
the score was around here."

"Oh yeah? What'd you tell him?"

"I said that we're an undercover branch of the Youth for the
Abolishment of Virginity Service gathering statistical data on the
shameful overabundance of nonerotic literature on the market."

"That should have turned him off," he chuckled.

"Hell no. I think he believed me," I answered half seriously.

"Well, see if you can't sell him a membership card or something."

"I don't know. He looks like the type who'd end up selling them to us."

"Hmm, organization . . ." Jerry shook his head and laughed sadly. "We'd make a pretty off-the-wall sort of union. Why doesn't he start with something comparatively simple like a sleepwalkers union?"

"I guess everybody's welcome to their own kick."

John dropped around the next day, and the day after that . . . and the day after that; so often did he drop around, in fact, that if he missed a day, someone would wonder where he was (which was as good as a membership card). He bided his time, surveying the situation and not saying too much until he was sure of his ground.

"What this group needs is *unity*," he would say occasionally. "With all these people, we ought to be able to do *something*."

"Oh? What would you suggest . . . a door-to-door anti–bubonic plague campaign?"

He wasn't given to answering questions of that sort but would sit clasping and unclasping his hands in perpetual nervous discontent while paraphrasing his convictions.

After his usual "lack of organization" prelude one evening, he came down to specifics: "You know, I been spending a lot of time thinking about this group—"

"As chairman in charge of our modest group, may I say that the honor is overwhelming," Jerry interrupted with mock pompousness.

"Oh, now look, man, this is serious. I've even got some plans drawn up." He produced a small pile of yellow lined papers. "I've worked with some other groups on this, but they fell apart before we could get anything done . . ."

"That seems to be indicative of something or other," Alan said dryly.

"Hear me out, will you? Here's the scene: Most of the people in this crowd are artists in one way or another, right? Right. So . . . we all get together, with proper organization, and form a colony . . ."

"What kind?" I inquired. "A leper colony?"

He shot me a look of intense displeasure, then began to elaborate on his scheme. His rapid, medicine showman—like manner of presentation and enthusiastic conviction began to tell, and the occasional jibes became fewer and less appreciated.

The magnificence of the idea was, to give due credit, infectious: a colony devoted to the preservation and nurture of artists (us) and their work. It was to be, as John outlined it, self-sustaining, self-governing, and the very incarnation of joy for all its devoted members. There was only one drawback: we had no cash ("Don't bother me with hassles yet . . . We'll get to things like that later," John said) nor any prospects for obtaining any. "So I suggest," he said, closing his presentation, "that we call a meeting together and pull in anyone who might be interested. Maybe," he added ominously, "we can get something going out of this scene before it's too late."

Suddenly, under John's impatient guidance, the group became "the Group" as a sense of belonging and direction weaved together the loose strings idly wrapped about one another. Meetings were held at which just about everything was decided except what in hell was going on.

John, the mysterious entity who had seemingly appeared out of nowhere, was indeed an organizing genius, and he went to work with a passion, organizing frantically. He gave Jerry the job of moderating the affair; Alan, he put in charge of the treasury

(?), and on my own head fell the position of secretary . . . so that not a gem would fall from their lips unheeded. I didn't have much to say about it; John handed me a pencil and a notepad with the words *Hard Core* written on the cover, then told me to get busy.

It took very little time to become completely enthused in the scheme. Besides . . . it was something to do, and that alone was rare enough.

For the next week, bloodshot eyes prevailed. The idea became all-encompassing and demanded full, unswaying attention. It began to shape itself in spite of us.

There was no time for sleep, only work, work, work . . . The coffee and Benzedrine flowed freely, and the amount of useless paperwork that eventually trickled from our half-conscious minds, through our pencils, and onto paper would have done a fair-sized corporation proud.

After the preliminary planning, open meetings were held to enthuse others with the idea.

"Now we've got to be careful about these meetings," John cautioned. "We can tell them just *so* much, no more . . . We don't want this thing to get out of hand. It's all right to get them enthusiastic enough to support us, you know . . . As a matter of fact, that's the purpose of the meetings, to raise funds. The rest of it we can handle ourselves . . ." I think he had some vague notion of spies or something on that order, but he had a way of being quite convincing, no matter what odd rules he might choose to lay down.

The funds, in the forms of pennies, nickels, and an occasional dime or quarter, came from nearly empty pockets; pockets that, though seldom graced with anything other than lint, were always open to ideals (or to the passing of a hat or a jug of wine).

The coins were deposited into an empty olive oil can whose weight, to our profound satisfaction, slowly grew to a considerable heftiness. The change probably remains in the can, wherever it may be, to this day . . . unless someone has seen fit to break the seal of trust that locked it from any purpose other than advancing the interests of the commune.

It was unanimously decided, after an hour or two of superfluous debate (requiring about eight pages of notes, later initialed, okayed, heaped in a stack on the floor, walked on, picked up, sifted through, rewritten, re-initialed, re-heaped, and somewhere later filed) to call the project the "Co-op" rather than the "Commune" because, as John said, "there's no reason to turn any unfavorable eyes on us. The locals already consider us to be a society of vagrants, degenerates, beatniks, and dope fiends. No use adding 'communists' to the list."

If the truth be known, with a few exceptions (notably Willy), our collective political knowledge and views were next to nonexistent. Besides being positively anti-HUAC (as who wasn't), anti-bomb (we had our own personal interests to consider), and anti–present administration (as who, in the history of mankind, hasn't been?), we more or less didn't give a collective damn about such goings-on in general.

The ordinary procedure was to hold a meeting and kick over unimportant trivia about goings-on in general until someone became intensely bored and would motion to close, and another observer, equally fatigued amid the endless flow of syllables, would second the motion.

The meeting would then break up, and the "hard core" (as we, the driving forces of the movement, numbering about five, fondly labeled ourselves) would retire to Stickney's, order a cup of coffee each, if we could afford it (the olive oil can was off-limits), then sit till daylight or ejection from the restaurant, whichever came first, and work on the *real* business.

The purpose of the meetings was to enthuse others with the idea, not, specially, to get anything concrete done. Anything of value (as it were) came from the hours of brainstorming in the restaurants. We would spread a multitude of papers across the table as the waitress eyed us furtively but helplessly, and begin work, occasionally clamoring for refills. As we worked, I was fond of bringing forth the concept that actually nothing was needed but money and that the organization would then take care of itself. I would receive a silent, bloodshot stare from John, the omniscient organizer, and the work would continue as though nothing had been said. One of us would occasionally drop out, of physical exhaustion, and sack out in the car for an hour or two, then come back and continue working.

When the time came, as it did every morning, when nothing came forth but babbles and occasional reiteration, we would retire en masse for a few hours and sleep.

Frustrating and impractical as it may sound, the idea was fascinating, though as ethereal as a pot of gold at the end of a rainbow, and would not be let go of; fascinating because it gave each of us a chance to prove to himself that he really *could* work rather than whiling away time at parties and endless waiting, as seemed our vocations. Alan's omnipresent enthusiasm was infectious; he never seemed to lose it. He was probably as aware, if not more, as we were that the Co-op was a gossamer dream, but he also knew the satisfaction we derived from the planning of it, and this was important to him. Alan derived his satisfaction from the pleasures of others, so he was not completely altruistic. I would realize this when, after bending over a notebook for half an hour, initialing, transcribing, passing on notes, I would look up to see Alan leaning back against his chair gently beaming, radiating that mysterious love which infallibly leaked through his British reserve toward his comrades in arms.

After several days of intensive work, the natural evolution became apparent to the rest of us. John's organization became half-hearted, though still functioning, for this was his medium.

Some of us wrote, some of us played instruments, some painted. John organized. When there was nothing immediate that required his talents, such as organization of a party, he would work on his manifesto, which was to change, naturally, in a period of several thousand years (he was most generous with time) the entire social structure of civilization.

John was that rarest combination of genes, the hardheaded, practical idealist. He would have loved nothing better than to be given the chance to organize the beauty of a sunset or the practical migration of birds. To John, organization was an art, and when there was nothing to organize, he would begin arranging his and our leisure hours (which were many). There was no harm in it, so we allowed him to organize unimpeded. Actually, there was no question of permission; it was a positive drive, and it was beautiful to watch. He would reduce anything under the sun to its lowest common denominator and work up until he had a complex organization going. It was common belief that John worked a half hour or so before going to bed every night, in order to organize his dreams.

He was tall and thin, with a Barrymore profile and a nervous disposition that allowed him little peace, except in sleep. His hands moved constantly and would weave the most fantastic designs in the air when he related a story.

It was a marvel to hear John relate something. His voice was rapid and eloquent, and he missed no possible point of interest when telling a story. He would say something that he considered comical, laugh, and without quite finishing the laugh, he was on to the next point of interest, his hands illustrating shapes, punctuation, amazement, and delight. What might have been annoying in a less fantastic individual was amazing in John. He would take the floor (interruptions were almost unheard of once he began) and relate stories of his days on the road: hopping freight trains, freezing on boxcars and gondolas, and living by his wits and con man—ship. All of this he would do with the characteristic leisureliness of a sportscaster in the final seconds of a big game.

John told of the lure of the train whistle; how it enters the blood and can never be quite forgotten. And he told of answering the call, often waking up in the middle of the night from a warm bed, putting a pack together, and starting off for places unknown before he was even quite awake; standing at the door of the boxcar on summer days, waving at the people he passed, dropping garbage in the Mississippi, and wearing the same leather jacket that his father had ridden the rails with before John was born.

And he told how a dude one day swiped the jacket from his father and how his father had retraced the bum's route, found him, retrieved the jacket, and left the dude in considerably worse shape than when he had found him.

And when he was finished, for the time being, he would sit down, fold his hands over his lean stomach, and smile until another wonderous story occurred to him.

When John slept, there was no question but that he *was* asleep. He slept as he organized: completely, fully, down to the last detail.

I have driven his car for hours as he slept in the makeshift bed he had built into the back (by removing the back seat and the lining of the trunk) only to have him awake at the end of the journey and ask if we were going somewhere.

John's car was an institution. He had sold it three times, but, like the fabled cat, it always returned through one quirk of fate or another. It had no hood, and the windshields were cracked. It would never run quite right for anyone but John, and it seemed to know when he was at the wheel.

John was indeed a rare individual, and it is fortunate that there was not another like him. They would have organized each other to death.

Jerry, in his unfathomable Jerryish way, kept things running smoothly. He was the indispensable dispensable man to the Co-op committee. Whether he added anything or not was of little importance; he was there, and it was his place to be there.

I sat and took everything in; this was my place, and I offered suggestions of remarkable import, which John would file under such headings as "trivia" or "things to be taken up at a later date" to keep me happy.

But Alan was the man who swung the axe. Alan the innovator, the driver, and the culminator. There was a vague possibility that this Utopian inner society might have emerged in spite of our careful planning had not Alan taken a trip to the Sierras for a month, to see some of America's natural wonders before returning to England and Cambridge. He sent occasional postcards from scenic points along the John Muir Trail, telling us that he was having a fine time, though rather footsore, and admonishing us to keep working. But these admonishments were not the same as Alan's presence, and we all felt a little ashamed at letting him down. However, our need for paperwork and organization (except, of course, for John) had vanished, and the Co-op died a death of exhaustion, as did so many of our dreams, and when Alan returned, moss was growing on its gravestone.

I WAS SITTING IN THE BOOKSTORE IDLY TEARING PIECES OF paper in half and then re-tearing the halves, dropping the shreds into a puddle of coffee that I had dribbled on the table for the purpose. Jerry played his guitar, his feet propped up on an adjacent table and his chair tilted back at an alarming angle. He would occasionally sing a song I knew, and I would sing along with off-the-wall harmonies.

David X. sat at the table next to us, a pack of cards arranged before him in neat rows. The rows curved slightly as a concession to the presence of Jerry's ill-shod feet in their midst. He moved the cards around from one pile to the other, twisting his beard in knots with his free hand. Diane sat next to him watching the moves intently and offering an occasional unsolicited suggestion.

David played patiently for a while, then stopped and looked Diane in the eye. "You know," he said, "I think I've discovered the essential thing every explorer should carry with him in case he ever gets lost at the South Pole or some out-of-the-way place like that."

"What's that?" asked his erstwhile kibitzer.

"A pack of cards. All he's got to do is spread them out in front of him and start playing solitaire. And just as sure as he

85

gets started . . . doesn't matter if he's five thousand miles from nowhere, someone's gonna come up behind him, start breathing down his neck, and tell him to put the black ten over the red jack."

Diane tried, unsuccessfully, to raise an eyebrow, then shifted her attention, with equal lack of success, to trying to get the guitar away from Jerry.

"Ha . . . women should be seen and not heard!"

"Oh, for God's sake, I just want to show you a new song I learned; it's not as though I were going to *keep* the guitar. You seem to forget that it's *my* guitar anyway."

"Tell me the name of the song and I'll sing it for you. I know every song ever written and most of them that weren't."

Diane, realizing that further entreating was useless, sighed and shifted her attention back to the card game.

Jerry continued to strum monotonously, momentarily uninspired. Jackson tried to follow the chord progression on his trumpet with little success. Every time he made a flagrant mistake, he would empty his spit valve as though it were responsible for the mistake rather than he.

"Mayhap you would be so kind as to play 'Hangman' again?" Jackson inquired, having worked out what he believed to be a satisfactory accompaniment to the song.

"Jesus, Jackson, I've already played it for you ten times."

Jackson rolled his eyes heavenward. "Peace, peace. Practice doth make cowards of us all. Pray tell, what hour is upon us?"

"It's about one," I answered, "calculating from the shadows."

"More about twelve," Jerry said.

"Or maybe three twenty," David added, looking up from his game.

"Halt, desist this attack upon my mental testii!" Jackson cried, getting up to search for a clock.

"Be sure to add an hour for standard time, then subtract it again, because we're on daylight saving time . . . I guess."

"Hey now, there's a sure cure for ennui!" Jerry exclaimed.

"What's that?" I asked.

"Change the time schedule every day. Drive people nuts, but it'd keep them occupied. Everyone would be so busy trying to find out what time it was that they wouldn't while away their dull moments inventing new kinds of bombs. It'd be a full-time job just figuring out when it was time to get off work."

"Aesthetically admirable, but unpractical in practical practice."

"Man, do I ever get ideas," Jerry went on. "Sometimes I think I'll never run out of ideas . . . all great, too. World-shaking ideas. It's just that no one ever seems to appreciate them for their true value. Well, that's humanity's fault, not mine. I do my best." He went back to strumming the guitar and singing "Lloyd George knew my father, Father knew Lloyd George" to the tune of "Onward, Christian Soldiers."

Just as most people are never seen without their clothes on, Jerry was never seen without a guitar. He was marvelously uninhibited about playing it and singing in his husky semi-tenor whenever the occasion presented itself (and even when the occasion did not present itself; he was too immersed in his art to worry seriously about occasions).

Alan and I had once accompanied him down the main street of town; Jerry decked out in his summer uniform of knee-length Levi's, a faded Ivy League shirt with an incredibly frayed collar, bare feet, and a wreath of leaves and vines twined jauntily through his seldom-cut locks. A borrowed guitar was slung over his shoulder, as usual, swinging from a length of brown wrapping twine (these were the days before Alan presented him with the "decadent" green braid cord, which, in turn, were before the not-too-distant days of a leather strap and four-hundred-dollar guitar).

It was not uncharacteristic that, as we walked down the street through crowds of weekend shoppers, Jerry decided to sing.

There are fleeting moments in which apparently minor decisions are to be made, but it is precisely in these seconds that the mode of thought which governs an entire life may be formed. This was one of those times. There was something so natural about singing at that moment; something so unencumbered by convention that I joined him rather than dropping back a few steps and looking innocuous.

And so it came to pass that we walked the main street of town, in the middle of the afternoon, singing about "Them Old Cotton Fields at Home" and whatever else came to mind; the warm California sun beating down on one of the many days upon which it would never rise again.

As we passed, people would avert their eyes as though afraid to admit the presence of such an enormous breach of etiquette . . . the same people who would pause for minutes to observe the twisted metal and broken glass of an automobile accident. But then, an auto wreck was more socially acceptable than we were. Social acceptance, however, did not hold a priority on our itineraries in those days, and so we sang. An occasional face would break from the drab blur of the crowd and grin as if to say, "I'd join you, but . . ." And some would raise their heads just a little higher with a "There but for the grace of God go I" expression, remaining otherwise unscathed. But then, who gave a damn . . . They were the same people who drank their wine from crystal glasses, instead of the dago red from cans and juice glasses, and we sang a little louder because we were one up on them.

We were different from other human creatures and knew it; reveled in it and eventually began to lose the distinction as we became too aware of it and time extracted its toll from youth. But a time of life that is an eternity in itself has no need for foresight and lives each day for itself; judging it on its own merits and letting it slip wherever time itself slips to, scarcely realizing that when a summer day dies, it is just as dead as any fly that has given up the ghost in a multitude of enticing spiderwebs.

We sat in our familiar haunt that night, continuing the day that was a continuation of the day before (and of the day before that); days with few goals other than their very living evident to the casual observer. Jerry and I were singing through our somewhat limited mutual repertoire, and I was trying to accompany his playing on a borrowed guitar. Every few songs, he would stop and introduce me to whomever might have wandered in: "This is Bob . . . Can't play guitar worth a damn, or sing much either, but what the hell, you need two people for a duet and he's handy. Not too bad on the tambourine, though."

"This is Jerry . . . He can play hell out of the back of the guitar with a couple of drumsticks, but he couldn't carry a tune if it was strapped to his back."

"Fortunately, we can carry it across, albeit by sheer force of stunning physical beauty and personality!"

"Sing something innocuous," Diane mumbled.

An elderly man with a flowing mustache was sitting in the corner, watching us with interest. When we had finished singing, he came over to our table.

"I'd like to talk to you boys for a minute, if you don't mind."

"Feel free. We're not proud," Jerry said.

He pulled up a chair and sat down. "I teach at Peninsula, a progressive elementary school across town, and I thought maybe you'd enjoy coming over for an assembly some Thursday morning and singing for the kids. We wouldn't be able to pay you anything, but I'm sure the kids would love to hear you if you have the free time."

If we had the free time . . . !

We went back to the room that night and began practicing in earnest. I started working on my own guitar playing, which was fair (though Jerry would not even acknowledge it *that* much; I promised to play very quietly, and besides, I did need a prop of some kind . . . He suggested a rubber band).

I began to feel professional about the matter; even to the point of picking up a couple of secondhand shirts, which Jerry flatly refused to wear. He couldn't have cared less; he would have been content to appear naked as long as they let him perform.

We were to give the show at ten thirty on a Thursday morning, and when the day rolled around, the first light of dawn found us practicing in order to get rid of our "morning voices." We got to the school bright and early to look the acoustics over and decide where to put the borrowed tape recorder (such a momentous performance could not very well go unrecorded for posterity).

The auditorium was in an old, dilapidated building that had once obviously been a mansion. It reeked of atmosphere and mildew. We tuned up and joked about how bad we were going to be, although we both knew that we would be glorious.

We had chosen a selection of songs that we thought would be apropos for grade school children (we later discovered a six-year-old tyke in the kindergarten class who knew all the songs we did and others so ethnic we had never even heard of them). As soon as the audience started to file in, Jerry's eyes lit up. He had been a little nervous about the whole affair, but when he realized that a good portion of his critics were scarcely three feet high, he became all smiles and benignancy. He understood the minds of children, because the workings of his mind, though in more abstract forms, so closely paralleled theirs.

The performance, though less than technically perfect, was embellished by Jerry's instinctive clowning, which to the kids more than made up for any inadequacies that the music might have had. They were perfectly attuned to Jerry and loved him from the start (and me, to a somewhat lesser degree; I had always been suspicious of kids, even when I was one).

After the concert, we were deluged by scores of small bodies that jumped upon our necks and clung to our legs. Jerry received six proposals of marriage, all of which he graciously accepted while trying to extricate himself from the melee.

We were pressured to stay the day and look around the school, becoming somewhat of a holiday. Since the school was run on anything but formal grounds, classes were dismissed so that the kids could go outside and sing with us on the unkempt lawn behind the buildings. We both decided, somewhere in the course of the afternoon, while being stuffed with bits and pieces of scores of lunches, that this was the only possible life: that of wayfaring minstrels.

This notion was further cemented into Jerry's mind by a little girl who had shyly offered him a small bronze brooch, which she told him was a medal for being the best singer in the world. He pinned it to his shirt and proudly wore it, telling everyone the story behind it, until he lost both the shirt and the brooch. He had a way of losing things (including a great deal of my meager belongings) that was almost supernatural.

A warm glow filled us as we left the school at the end of the day. Jerry had no comprehension that there might exist anyone who would not be enchanted by our performing. My convictions, though existent, were not on par with Jerry's ideal world. It was a world that I later began to see fray at the cuffs, like his omnipresent faded shirt, but never unravel completely. It was a child's garden, but a garden slowly beginning to grow over with weeds that he did not understand and so chose not to acknowledge the existence of.

He understood the law of cause and effect because that is a necessity, but not the reasons behind it, and if he trod on toes, it was not from malice but because the concept that there were toes other than his had not fully entered his mind. As he began to comprehend these things, he began to "grow up." All the while, people prodded him to mature (and then lost patience with him when he did). They urged him and pushed him out of his world into another, their own, which he could not fathom, and he began to lose the desire to understand until, suddenly, he found himself back in his own world, only to find that during his absence the weeds had choked the flowers and the sky was no longer limitless but a roof that loomed ever lower, threatening to crush whatever brave trees dared to grow.

He tried to transfer his garden to the "real" world and would occasionally appear in a battered blue hat, claiming that it was a "magic hat" and would allow no one but magical people to wear it, or to walk with his magic cane. And Jerry's magical people would often believe him and think that perhaps they really *were* magical in some way that they had never perceived, and would love Jerry for letting them know about it; shielding him and feeding him in hopes that he would allow them to remain magical.

When he became aware of their ulterior motives, he would abruptly take up his magic stick, disillusioned, and go elsewhere in his search for someone to push back the sky so that he could again live in his garden.

The real magic lay in Jerry himself, for few things were so ugly or hopeless, in those days, that he could not detect a glimmer of reflected magic in them. It is a quality one loses when one comes abruptly face-to-face with an adverse world and allows its petty jealousies and trivialities to sting more deeply than they should; a world that he eventually recognized, but in the very recognition of which meant that it was too late to run back, for all gates but one were quietly closed.

I had been writing, off and on, determined to devote full-time to the pursuit as soon as I had gathered enough experience to be able to write something worthwhile, but this ethereal goal dwindled to a spark as we practiced diligently through the greater part of our waking hours during the weeks to come.

Gradually, out of the hours of practice, we developed a feeling for each other's sense of harmony; the important knowledge of exactly what note to hit in any given melody line. As our harmony grew tighter, we also began to develop an unconscious philosophy in our singing: to knock down all the walls except communication. If harmony got in the way, we would work it over and modify it until we felt that we had extracted whatever it was that a song is supposed to convey. And then, with a tidy repertory under our belts, we were ready for something to happen.

Something happened in the form of a concert at a local university, for which we were to be paid a nominal fee. The opportunity fell into our laps, as did most of our opportunities. Opportunity came in the person of Shad, whom we had once picked up hitch-hiking in the remains of my battle-worn Chrysler (sans rods, sans brakes, etc.). He had "turned on" to us and had become a familiar figure at the bookstore. He looked oddly paradoxical among us: the clean-cut ideal of wholesome college youth associating with what must have looked like the bearded scrapings from the bottom of the nonrestricted social register.

One afternoon, he came bounding into the bookstore. "Say, you guys want to sing at my house? I told the guys about you, and they think it'd be great!"

Several weeks later, the campus was covered with posters, designed by Jerry and executed on silk screen by Shad. We spent a day hitting every likely spot with a poster and masking tape.

Barbara, a constant companion who, in later days, was to become a pivot point in Jerry's quest, became our patron. She gave us the use of a rumpus room behind her house to practice in and then sat back, unnervingly critical, while Jerry and I fought it out over points of musical conflict such as: "You're full of it, Bob. We can't sing a song like that in front of a college audience."

"Hell we can't. We've got to give them something to identify with. I don't care if every other group in the country does sing it."

"Identify? What do you think you are, an advertising executive?"

Barbara would usually mediate at this point, thus saving an hour of arguing over which Jerry would usually rise triumphant by sheer force of perseverance and lung power.

The afternoon before the concert, things suddenly began to go wrong. The guitars refused to stay tuned, and our ears became hypersensitive to anything that was the faintest bit "off." Jerry became more convinced than ever, in fact downright adamant, that I should switch my instrumental efforts to rubber bands and/or finger snapping. He also feared that he was coming down with laryngitis and other exotic diseases of the throat. We finally decided to give up practicing altogether for the rest of the day and take our chances with what we had already accomplished.

We picked Barbara up that evening. She had tailored the two shirts that I had bought for the other concert into a casual-professional sort of affair. Needless to say, in our hypertense condition, they could not be expected to fit. Jerry put his on and its pastel green dampened immediately with sweat.

I had sung before audiences before, in the army, so I had a degree of composure. I talked encouragingly on the way, but Jerry mumbled, "Save your voice. You'll need it later."

The concert was due to begin at seven, and it was suddenly six fifty-five, and we still had another three miles to drive.

"That's all right," I said cheerfully. "Shows always start at least ten minutes late. Gives the audience a chance to settle down."

Jerry muttered something pregnant under his breath, and Barbara flushed silently. It started to rain.

"Aha, an evil omen," said Jerry. By the time we reached our destination, it was raining hard. I pulled my Chrysler into the closest parking lot, and we got out and ran for the building, shielding our instruments with our bodies. Shad met us at the door.

"Hey, I thought you guys had decided not to come."

"Is it too late to change our minds now?" asked Jerry.

"Afraid so." He showed us to a small room where we could tune up. Barbara came in with us and tried to be soothing while the guitars refused to tune properly. I drank voluminous amounts of water. My throat had become inexplicably dry. I peeked out the door, which afforded a view of a small part of the room we were to perform in. "There's hardly anybody there!"

We cleared our throats several times, drank some more water, then bravely, with a forced casualness, we went in. Suddenly the "hardly anybody there" became a vast sea of faces. Shad went up front and introduced us glowingly while I said a fervent novena in hopes that we could live up to our introduction.

Jerry put the guitar strap around his neck and adjusted the weight of the new twelve-string guitar Barbara had bought us for the occasion. He shot me a quick, heartfelt "what have we got to lose save face?" look and launched into the base run of "Santy Ano."

We're sailin' down the river to Liverpool,
Heave away, Santy Ano,
Round Cape Horn to Frisco Bay,
Way out in Californi-o.

My mouth was very dry, and my tongue seemed to adhere to the roof of it. As we sang, I looked around at the audience. Their faces seemed exceedingly long, as though they were there to judge us rather than to listen.

So it's heave 'er up and away we'll go,
Heave away, Santy Ano,

The harmony blended as it always had, but it seemed to echo hollowly across the room, reverberating with unpleasant overtones.

Heave 'er up and away we'll go,
Way out in Californi-o . . .

I had an empty, giddy feeling in my stomach as Jerry replayed the bass run to wind up the song. Then, wonder upon wonders, there was applause. That was all that was needed. The look of determination and do-or-die left Jerry's face, and I relaxed perceptibly. A glow overtook him as he settled back into the swing of things, and he began to introduce the songs with whatever came off the top of his head: "This next number is an old Indian work song, translated from the original Slavic by the head of the Hebrew department at Sacred Heart University . . ."

Time seemed to pass rapidly, and suddenly we had finished the first half of our program.

"Well," I said, "do you think we ought to pack up and git while the gittin's good?"

"Hell no. Let's hear what they have to say."

We split and mingled, ready to hear the verdict. Barbara came up to me, her face aglow. "You were both just great. I've never heard you better!"

"Huh?" I said numbly. Suddenly, it began to filter through that we had not been as bad as I thought. I went into our tune-up room and drank several glasses of water while trying to reassemble my nerves. Jerry came in and repeated the process.

"Well, what do you think?" I asked.

He gargled the water around his throat, then spit it in the sink. "You were great."

"No, it was you. You were marvelous."

"Far be it from me to accept the credit for your glorious performance . . ."

"Oh, hell. Let's go back and gas 'em some more before the spell wears off."

"Quite."

The intermission ended; we started up again. I was mildly surprised to see everyone still there, ready to hear more. I suddenly felt a wave of affection for the unknown faces who were allowing us to show our stuff and actually seemed to be enjoying the whole affair. A few who sat in the back with die-hard critic looks on their faces began to soften, and they took on the more relaxed mood of enjoyment.

By the time we ended with "Down by the Riverside," everyone in the place was singing along with the choruses. Jerry was exuberant, and shouted between choruses, "Everybody sing now!" and "I can barely hear you!" and other devices designed to help them drown us out, and they responded:

I'm gonna lay down my sword and shield,
Down by the riverside,
And study war no more . . .

When we were finished, they wanted more. I felt as though I weighed twenty pounds, and the applause rang in my ears long after we left. It was like a drug, only more addictive than any yet conceived in the smoky depths of any opium den. This was life, and life was a fascinating, exhilarating thing.

There was a party for us afterward, and we drifted in late, still barely aware of which planet we were on. I sat down in a corner with a glass of red wine and watched people dance and talk and laugh. I was suddenly in love with people in all shapes and sizes as I sat there nodding to the music and digging things intensely.

A girl was dancing by herself near me, drifting and moving her arms in rhythm to "Sketches of Spain." She seemed to be drawn completely into the wailing tones of Miles's trumpet, swaying and bending, changing as the mood of the piece changed. I had noticed her often before. Her face was Grecian, sharply chiseled and softened with pale blue eyes that never seemed to quite focus on any particular object but looked instead, with an innocent wonder, at something just over the horizon of consciousness. Her long blond hair, a living moving part of her, flowed gently with her body as she danced. She was not tall, but her carriage gave the impression that she was so. There was a fluid lightness in every movement of her body. She was not dancing *to* the music but rather becoming one with it. I watched fascinated until the music stopped. She stood still for a moment, as though cut suddenly from the life-giving source. She sat down near me. "Hello, Darjeeling," I said. I made the name up on the spur of the moment.

"Hi. I liked your concert very much," she answered.

"Thank you," I replied, wanting painfully to say something witty or intelligent, but failing. "I'm glad you did."

"Jesus, Bob, you sing 'Man of Constant Sorrow' like an operatic aria. It's a Southern mountain song, for God's sake."

"What do you want me to do, sing it like I just had my throat operated on, the way you do?"

Jerry looked exasperated. "Look, that's the way it's *supposed* to be done . . . Listen to Mike Seeger or the Carter Family do it."

"Well, goddamn it, I'm neither the Carter Family *or* Mike Seeger. If you want to do it like a damned hillbilly, you can do it alone."

He looked thoughtful for a moment, then: "I've been thinking about that, Bob."

I was startled. "What d'you mean?"

He sat down on the desk, scrutinizing the sound hole of his guitar. Then he looked up. "It doesn't swing, I mean. I . . . well, hell! That's just it; it doesn't swing anymore, not the way I want it."

"Big thing to say . . . Why?"

He ran his fingers across the frets, picking out the runs of "Man of Constant Sorrow," stopping partway through to retune an errant string. "Well, you know the 'walls' you talk about knocking down? It seems to me we did pretty well for a while; we've got all those down, but there are new ones."

"New ones?"

"Well, frankly, I feel like I'm being held back. Not that we don't hit it off pretty well as a duet, but that's established now; in fact . . . stagnating. I want to move ahead. You've got your writing, man, and you're not doing too bad from what I've seen . . . but the singing is a pastime for you . . . Anyway, it's what I want to do. It's kind of hard to explain, so I won't go into it, but I feel like we've come to a standstill, or at least I have. 'Santy Ano' and 'Cotton Fields' are fine in their way, but they just scratch the surface. I've been studying and reading . . . listening, and I'm just beginning to find out how near the surface they are. It's an art, Bob, one that will take a long time to learn well, but that's what I want to do. So . . ." He scratched the strings, then put down the guitar.

"So . . . I guess I understand. It doesn't even surprise me too much, really. Anyway, good luck, you know."

He clasped my shoulder. "Thanks."

I sort of half smiled. It seemed the appropriate thing to do. "Want to make it down to the coffeehouse or something?"

"No; I've got work to begin."

"Right. See you later."

I WALKED TOWARD THE COFFEEHOUSE WITH A VAGUE, EMPTY feeling in the pit of my stomach. Something important had suddenly dropped out, and in its place was a feeling of bewilderment; a carousel stripped of its music while the horses continued to glide, phantomlike, around the never-ending track.

I WAS SITTING AT MY TYPEWRITER, INTENTLY TRYING TO PRO-
duce something of any character at all, encountering only
frustration. Suddenly, the door flew open. "Christ," I muttered, "not another distraction."

"Heh heh," said the intruder, stroking his beard and grinning
secretively. "Betcha can't guess what I have in this box."

"An elephant?"

"Close, but not quite!" He waved the tiny cardboard box.

"Three elephants? Green ones?"

"Right!" He opened the box.

"Gather round, kiddies. Heh heh." He produced first one, then
two, then three slender cigarettes, tightly rolled in brown paper.

"Such wickedness shall not go unheeded."

The ceremony over, we commenced to dispose of the "elephants" in rapid succession, eating the bits that were left over as
they flamed out.

"Boss, boss," Alan murmured, exhaling a thin cloud of sweet
smoke.

"Hoha," John answered, looking as though he had a 50 percent
head start on us, passing the "joint" and trying to hold his breath
at the same time.

Simultaneous with the swallowing of the last shred of evidence, the door opened and Willy came in. "Hi, brothers," he said, grinning broadly.

He was answered by a chorus of sinister giggles. The dense, pungent smell of the room left no doubt as to the nature of our condition. He was slightly in his cups, so he took the news that he had missed out on some real boss stuff quite well. He sat back and prepared to enjoy the forthcoming show.

"Dig this," said Jerry, getting up and attempting to play Ravel's "Daphnis and Chloé" on the record player. He tried to put the needle down on the beginning groove but was having quite a bit of trouble with it.

John and Alan floated around the room, turning out lights and lighting a string of Christmas lamps we had hanging about the room.

The significant characteristic of the "high" we were on is a heightened degree of suggestibility, commonly referred to as "tripping out." It is a state similar to dreaming . . . a state of infinite perception of minutiae. The choral strains of "Daphnis and Chloé," with abrupt changes of mood, set the scene beautifully. I felt a sudden urge to run to the typewriter to catch the scene. I sat down and could not quite remember what it was I had intended to write about. I decided to start with the Gettysburg Address.

Fourscore and seven years ago our fathers brought forth on this continent a new nation conceived in 19gtrty and dedicated to the frustration a new nation conceived in liberty and ded9cated to the preposition that all men is crested ee shit eq7al eaul or dual pu pipez godam it pipes.

Wither forth art thou headed my deares mother for the regions which lie out south of the fourscore region of the Apocalypse and reiterate the first movement, fourscore and sever years out country so, in the interim I would like to say that the main and only reason for the gratification of the people in understanding the realization of our self reinterest. I do not seem to understand the relation ship between this and your father, but I can still remember sincerely yours, your Mama many kissesxxxx

Below this, which I discovered beside the typewriter the next day, was written a fragment of dialogue:

"What do you mean god runs around naked? I don't give a damn if he is a spirit, he's got to wear clothes. It's all a part of the image, man. What in hell do you think they'd say in some self-respecting church if you ran in and shouted god runs around naked?"

When I returned from the typewriter, Jerry and Alan were facing each other, waving their hands hypnotically and mouthing indistinguishable words. Willy turned on the electric heater and said, "Don't you guys think you ought to get in out of the cold?"

Suddenly, we realized that it was very cold, and so we crowded around the roaring fireplace. I rubbed my hands together to get the circulation started again. Jerry sat looking very intent as the music from the phonograph rose and lulled.

"Have I ever told you about my visit to the Land of Here and Now?" he asked with a wistful expression on his face; his eyes staring, unfocusing, into the great fire.

"Many years ago, I was walking up a golden staircase, when I saw something glittering on the step ahead of me. I tried to get it, but it kept moving up another step. I followed it . . . It seemed to be luring me into a room that was at the very top of the staircase . . . only it wasn't the top, because when I got there, I saw another staircase beyond. I went into the room, and there, before my eyes, were millions of the brightest shining things. I tried to pick them up, but they flowed through my fingers like water . . ."

His voice was hypnotic. The simple story seemed to take hours to tell and held us spellbound with a remarkable fascination. The holes and loose threads were filled in by our own imaginations.

"Suddenly, I felt a hand touch my shoulder softly, and a golden voice seemed to drift across the fields of time. 'Do you know where you are?' it said. 'You are in the seldom-realized Land of Here and Now.'"

His story completed, he continued to stare into the "fire." "I'll never forget that as long as I live . . . I was actually there for a few moments . . . actually *there* . . ." A look of great sadness filled his eyes.

Forgetting about the cold, we later went out to dig the rotation of the universe. A dog barked in a garage, from which we conjured, mentally, a pack of vicious wolves.

"Wolves . . . Head for cover!" John shouted, and we went scurrying back out of the night into the safety of the room.

I felt another urge to start writing. I sat down and rolled a sheet of paper into the typewriter. The others noticed my preoccupation and crept up behind me. Suddenly, they were all around me. "Your typewriter has legs!" Jerry shrieked. "How can you write on a typewriter with legs?"

"Nothing but run-on sentences, horrible . . . horrible," Alan murmured. I felt as though a vast multitude of people were behind me, pointing at me, screaming at me, trying to distract me. Over all came the music, the moods of which tinted the whole scene. By a tremendous effort of will, I blanked them out of my mind and began to write furiously. Every movement of my fingers was sharp and defined, but yet, slow as I seemed to be working, I could not seem to speed up. It was as though my mind were divorced from physical time, yet my body had to obey its dictates.

And for a moment, it was glorious. They stood about me as I tried to write, digging my typewriter for a few minutes. Then they tripped out over an elephant that had just entered the door and left me alone for a while.

I have been smoking the same cigarette for an hour, it seems, and yet it is only half-gone when I look at it.

I am on a solitary kick now. I hear the action going on behind me, but I feel detached from it.

They notice me every once in a while and try to throw me into another trip, but I resist. A resistance trip. The chorale voices of Daphnis and Chloé . . . magical vibrance. I hear the crashing of cymbals . . . of thunder . . . I can't write fast enough to describe it . . . it disappears. Someone is turning the lights off and on, and I lose my train of thought.

The music has a galloping theme now . . . Christ, why can't I write the beauty . . . I have been writing forever . . . the clink of the bell and return of the carriage. I feel the beauty, but my fingers will not move fast enough to describe it. Willy keeps fooling with the record player and speeding it up. Humanity . . . speed the tempo of passion. Disconnected . . . I try not to be disconnected, yet they are insistent.

I left for a moment, but I was drawn back, back to this typewriter. A trip, of course, but . . . there it goes again, the chorale, the whisper of the forest . . . the breath of a dawn or perhaps a sunset. A tower of mystic passion—the willow. The gods whisper through my mind, through my mind . . . the pipe of Pan wailing through the shrubbery of the Mount of Olives . . . or through a forest glade where the quiet pond reveals unto him the face of Narcissus . . . and the pipe of Pan . . . now soft, now compelling, wafts . . . wafts and the voice of angels breaks through the summer's day . . . or perhaps spring.

The pace of the music changes, and I jump up to put the beauty back . . . to capture the mood.

The mood is within me . . . flashes against my breast . . . the torrent of Jove thunders for but an instant, and then is stilled with the gentle breeze from the soft blue mountaintop.

A valley . . . I feel the winding stream flow sweetly, gently, but I feel the torrent within its womb swell and begin to grow. How can the senses be so dull as not to see the beauty in this other than when influenced . . . Jerry's seldom realized world of Here and Now.

Again the passion, the mighty roar, the crash, and then . . . gentle beauty, a murmur . . . the pipe of Pan again.

Oh, hold me fast in that wonderland for but a life, and Christ . . . the tempo changes . . . I must start it over again . . . back it must go . . . forever back until the simple truth and power of beauty again hold the rapturous key to heaven before heaven.

Transient youth, enfold to thy breast the searched-for grail, and know it to be nothing but that which it is.

Jerry came up behind me. "Hey, man, do you know the difference between a rabbit and an Easter egg?"

"No, what's the difference between a cabbage and an illiterate?"

"A counterfeit five-dollar gold piece." He sat down and cracked up profusely. Then he ran to the door and flung it open.

"It's spring!" he announced (although it was quite dark). "Look at the flowers blooming . . . the birds are singing. God, it's wonderful to be out in the fresh air again after being snowbound all winter!"

A child would not understand the ecstasy of our state, for a child is in it perpetually, until his senses become dulled with reason. But for a time, we experienced the lost joy of "playing"; the all-encompassing world of a fairy tale. For a few moments, my friends became my "playmates," for there is no hypocrisy in the world of a child.

When I awoke the next morning, I looked through the sheets of paper that I had written the night before (part of which are transcribed here, unedited) and was amazed at the lack of restraints and formula in what I had done. Parts were pure nonsense, but some of the papers had the flow, the tranquility, the passion, and the pure observation that the conscious mind seems obliged to edit, which seldom escapes, intact, from the subconscious.

Fair the pipes are playing,
And lolling through the fields and the meadows,
Brisk in the autumn silence
And the ruffle of new blown grass against your legs
The flash of sun upon thy cheek.
The voices cry forth,
The forest tingles and drops of crystal bestir its leaves,
Swelling from the heart,
The torrent of glory,
No, softness,
Or . . . light, fair upon the end of summer.

Pipe of Pan, wail through the glades of thy
Soft still forest . . .
Where the tree weeps beside the riverbank,
A land of fairytale and gods of this earth.
The choir of the winds sails upon the silvery sun of noon,
Through a glade of mystic dreams,
Passion
And the softness beyond soft.

"O wad some Power the giftie gie us
To see oursels as ithers see us!
It wad frae mony a blunder free us,
An' foolish notion . . ."

—Robert Burns, "To a Louse"

THERE WAS AN ANTICIPATION IN THE AIR, EVEN MORE SO than usual. It seemed as though the ceaseless waiting that had held us fast in its lethargic grasp during the last few months was about to resolve into something tangible. The smoke-filled atmosphere of the room seemed pregnant with promise. I felt that I was on the threshold of something; something I was not too sure of . . . but something that was bound to break soon.

All of us had talked that night about what seemed to be coming. The feeling of tension was a mutual thing: a contagious sort of mass hypnosis demanding resolution, ready to create one out of its own being if nothing corporal appears to fill its desires. The overture was mysterious; we knew nothing and yet we knew. And we talked, not just in words but in *communication*, that rare form of understanding that sometimes slips unheralded into a conversation. Communication . . . the fascination of which precludes sleep or hunger or anything except further communication.

Alan sat in the corner of the room, chair tilted back against the wall, feet propped on the desk. John had been organizing something or other, but his notebook lay closed on the floor.

The Blind Prophet hung, slightly off center, as usual, on the wall and seemed to partake fully in the communication; the

117

mysterious, omnipresent Prophet who seemed to know so much about us and yet held a tactful silence. I had heard people talk about the Prophet's artist occasionally, but the subject seemed to be avoided when possible, as though it brought back memories that were better unrecalled. I knew that both Jerry and Alan had been in the accident in which he was killed, and there seemed to be a mutual unspoken agreement not to mention it.

That night, though, it did not seem out of place to bring up any subject. It was as if all the cages had been opened and the wild animals freed; allowed to forage for themselves in the manner of instinct.

"What kind of person was he?" I asked Jerry, looking toward the Prophet.

Jerry continued to strum the guitar as though he hadn't noticed the question. A few moments later, he answered. "It's kind of hard to sum a person up in a few words, but the closest I can come is 'odd.' He was quiet sometimes and loud at others, like everyone else, but he seemed to know something we didn't. He seemed to know he was going to die soon . . . he even joked about it as though it were a foredrawn, unalterable fact. I remember him talking about it the night it happened.

"We were having a party in somebody's apartment, and we decided to move it up to the Chateau. It turned out pretty quiet, and some of us were sitting in front of one of Paul's new paintings he had leaning against the fireplace. It was one of his conductor series. You've seen them, haven't you?"

"A couple of them." I had seen an exhibition of Paul's work, part of which was a series of conductors, executed in characteristic swirling dark colors. One painting in the exhibition had particularly drawn my attention. It was labeled *Death and the Artist* and was a self-portrait of Paul working on a canvas. A figure of the Grim Reaper, which seemed to melt into the dark background, pointed a skeleton finger at the canvas within the canvas. I passed on to the other paintings in the exhibit but found myself coming back to *Death and the Artist* several times. Though I didn't know who the artist was, at the time, the painting seemed to symbolize that very casual acceptance of death that Jerry said Paul had exhibited.

"The conversation got around to life and death, and while we were talking, Alan suddenly grabbed a poker from the fireplace and pointed it at Paul, pretending to be Death. Paul laughed and cringed back as though he were an old man suddenly confronted with fate. He went around like that for a while, until the humor wore off.

"I remember Jackson was blowing his horn, and nobody was listening, like always. It was just like any other party at the Chateau. There was this one guy there I didn't know. I think his name was Gary . . . Anyway, when he saw Paul acting like that, he turned kind of pale and began saying the weirdest kind of things. He was sitting there telling when people would enter the room and who they'd be, and he said he felt that something was going to happen and narrowed it down to me, Alan, Paul, and Lee, the guy that drove us home. He kept telling everyone to drive easy as they left, but he didn't say anything when we went. I saw him again afterward, and he said it was as though something were holding his throat, not letting him say anything.

"Paul said he had to be at work early, so Alan and I decided to ride home with him and come back later.

"We were all feeling high, and we went pretty fast down the back road behind the school. Paul said the speed was 'marvelous' and kept telling Lee to step on it. He kept saying it, and we went faster and faster. I don't know what happened, exactly, but the car started to skid to the right and went over the dividers. We were all thrown out . . . except Paul. I didn't know what had happened to him, but we had smashed up right across from the veterans' hospital.

"I'll never forget the way people were standing out front and looking out windows, but nobody did anything. My nose was broken and I was bleeding all over, and the people just stood there and watched.

"All you have to do is have that experience once, man, and you never want to be one of those people who just stands there hoping to see someone messed up so they can go home and tell everyone how sick it made their poor, sensitive souls. They just stood there, not doing a damned thing. I finally got up and walked over to the hospital and reported the accident myself . . ."

"Did they pull you right into the emergency room?"

"No," he laughed. "As a matter of fact, I went into the waiting room and sat down and read a magazine while they called up the emergency hospital a couple of miles away. I must have been out of my head from shock . . . I just sat there and looked through *Life* until somebody came and told me to get in the ambulance.

"But you know what was really odd? That guy I told you about, Gary . . . On his way home from the party, he had to stop while an ambulance went past. He said later that he knew right away who was in it."

"Jesus," I said while Jerry went back to strumming guitar. He played for a while, then set it down.

"I guess that's the closest I've ever come to death. It shakes you up, but it makes you realize things that are so obvious you might go through a whole life and never notice them. Alan and I were damned lucky; we were just laid up in the hospital for a couple of weeks. Time to think and rearrange things. It made me realize that I could never be sure where I'd be tomorrow, or even if I'd be alive. That's why I'm living like I am now, doing what I want to do instead of working away at some job to establish the security for a tomorrow I might never be around to see."

"And then there's a love thing," Alan added. "We all feel it sometimes, but we're afraid to say it, and sometimes we wish we'd said it when it's too late to. When you suddenly realize how close you came to losing your last chance or how suddenly you might lose it, it's time to start reworking your values."

"That's how this group really began . . . I mean, as more than a social clique," Jerry said. "A lot of us seemed to realize this, and it drew us closer together. It all happened just before you came around. You missed the game, but you got the score, though. That's the thing that counts in the end."

And so we sat there, the four who had seen the scene "mature"; the four who were one day to willingly, though with due appreciation, acknowledge its disintegration, and we talked.

As the night rolled on, we communicated of life, of direction, and of the scene. Our walls were lowered. John, the organizer, the "hard core," came forth, and Alan, observer and commentator, abandoned the vestiges of his British reserve, and the room glowed with life; life and the wonder of it as seen by those who had begun to question it, only to find that one answer, like Jason's beast, gave birth to endless others, while the Golden Fleece hung just out of reach. Love was the essence of it, and a sense of kinship touched each of us. We felt it and were not embarrassed by it, though it is the sort of thing that cannot quite withstand the harsh light of scrutiny (and these things are prone, in time, to scrutiny) and must draw back into the shadow in the stark fire of day. Once conceived, however, it is always present, though often awaiting a more twilight hour to reappear.

We adjourned in the small hours of the morning and drove John's amazing car to an all-night restaurant, where we sat till near dawn, as we had often done, over a single cup of coffee each. As we talked, I was amazed to find that I, who observed so much, had been myself observed, and now the reports were coming in. I listened, at first uncomfortably, then eager, for my walls were down and I could step outside and look inward critically.

And so the night progressed until the sun rose with a pale might and filtered through the fog. We drove back to the room and sat at the window watching the day begin. The fog dispersed and the sunlight glinted on the windows of sleeping houses, then, ascending, glistened about the dew-moist meadow across the road, eliciting a haze of tinkling morning colors from millions of tiny mirrors, each throwing full force into the show before being seduced back into the clouds to await another performance.

It was that time of day that one can appreciate fully only by keeping vigil over the night, watching with a mind unclouded by sleep.

The Prophet watched with us, the uncomplaining guest who watched over us from day to day, over our depressions and jealousies, our days and our nights, our beauty and occasional ugliness. He to whom all goals and ideals stood naked, allowing them to judge themselves, for what other judge can determine so harshly, yet so truly, as Self?

There was no time for sleep, for the shape of the earlier anticipation was becoming clear. Alan had realized it for what it was and later tagged the occurrence "the love scene."

There was no better way to describe it, for what other emotion can one feel when he senses a kinship of minds so strong as to seem nearly palpable?

It was like a disease. Once the mind was infected with it, the symptoms became readily apparent . . . communication, understanding, and a desire to share the feeling.

My mind was crystal clear, and I saw things as I had never seen them before; most important, I began to realize myself. I had been frantically searching for a direction, some meaning to my life over and above parties and eating, sleeping and existing . . . waiting. I had no time for concessions to sleep and hunger. When my eyes began to close in spite of me, I would drink more coffee or down a stimulant in order to allow my body to keep pace with my state of mind.

Days and nights suddenly began to blur into a vast continuum that I felt outside of as universes untouched began to form in my consciousness. Hunger vanished completely, and I began to forget what sleep felt like; I had no use for it. Sleep was a sinister intruder who clouded my mind and gobbled up years of my life. The future, which heretofore had seemed to stretch outward to infinity, suddenly appeared terminable.

I did not become fully aware of the demands I was making on my body until the fourth night, when I attended a concert. A folk singer was appearing, one whom I had wanted to see for some time. All I can remember is that she sang a few songs before the most marvelous things began to occur onstage. Her face would disappear and be replaced alternately by those of people I knew, dressed in brilliant raiment. Her guitar would occasionally change into a grand piano, but the sounds came through unaltered. The grand finale came as the clouds opened up and the snow began to fall and drift across the stage. The singer became a little old lady, clad in wretched rags, singing for alms in the driving blizzard.

After the performance, I went back to the room and wrote feverishly, trying to capture the crystalline quality of my mind on paper. My physical senses were distorted from fatigue, but my mind seemed vivid and alert.

After writing for an eternity, I stood up to stretch and brush away the cobwebs that were forming on my body. There was a dull, persistent ache in my back, and the base of my neck complained of the intolerable weight of my head. My vision suddenly began to disappear in a whirling mass of black. I sat down and shook my head violently. When my vision cleared, I found myself in a garden. There was a heady fragrance in the air that drifted around in bluish clouds. I was staring at a wall. I looked around and saw that the entire garden was enclosed by similar walls. There was a small fault in one of them through which a stream gushed, winding erratically through the garden and out through a similar fault in another wall. It suddenly occurred to me that I had been in the garden for an intolerably long time.

A pale blue light seemed to emanate from everything; a giddy phosphorescence. I was sitting on an ornate bench under which twisted vines of ivy. The vines had entwined around my ankles, and I could see them slowly growing higher. Annoyed, I reached down to disentangle myself. They tore easily from the ground, leaving small puddles of red liquid as I pulled them up. When I had uprooted all of them, I threw them into a small pile. The vines began to slowly disentangle from one another and push their roots back into the ground. I stomped my heel into the midst of them, but they sprang back, resilient as rubber.

The wall nearest me, the one through which the stream emerged, glowed with a vibrant heat that seemed to penetrate and warm the garden. I had an uncontrollable urge to get away from the annoying ivy; to climb the wall and look over, for I had no idea as to what lay on the other side. I ran to the wall and tried to look over. It was too tall, so I tried to climb it but found that it was too slippery and offered no handholds. I sat down and thought for a while, then decided to try the wall through which the stream vanished. As I approached the other wall, I felt a vague unease but was determined to try it. The closer I came to the wall, the greater became my uneasiness. As I touched the wall, a sudden icy chill coursed through every nerve. I snatched my fingers away. They were stained a dull black where they had been in contact with the wall. It seemed to be a sheet of solid ice that loomed threateningly above my head. I had a sudden, unreasoning fear of it and backed away. I turned to run, but the ground suddenly had the quality of gum, and each frantic step consumed minutes.

When I finally reached the other wall again, its radiance seemed to quiet the fear I had experienced at the ice wall. I pressed my body against it to warm myself. It yielded slightly. My curiosity mounted to the point where I had to get over and find out what was on the other side. I could no longer stand being anywhere near the strange wall through which the river disappeared. As hard as I tried, I could find no method for engaging the climb.

Looking hopelessly about me, my eye was drawn to the crevice through which the stream entered the garden. It looked large enough to squeeze through. As I entered the crevice, I pressed myself tightly against the side, not wanting to touch the water. I found that I had entered a long tunnel. At the far end gleamed a brilliant light that seemed to draw me toward it. I inched my way through until I could no longer stand the suspense. I started to run, soaking my bare feet in the stream as I ran. I ran for hours, not seeming to make any progress until finally I fell, breathless.

I closed my eyes and tried to regain my wind. When I opened them again, I found myself on the other side of the wall. All that I could see was a vast plane stretching into the distance. It was perfectly flat, and no object of any kind, no shadow, marred its blankness. An unfathomable distance away, a deep blue-black sky joined the plane. As I stared, I suddenly realized that it was not the sky at all but an immense tidal wave that was crashing toward me.

I could not run; there was nowhere to run to. The foamless wave began to cover the plane. I backed up until I touched the wall. Then I noticed a boat lying on the ground next to the crevice. I pushed it quickly into the stream and jumped in.

The bottom of the boat was covered with a sticky resin, the color of that which had dribbled from the ivy plants. It oozed around my body as the boat started to drift back into the tunnel. I tried to extricate myself, succeeding only in sticking more fast to the gummy substance. The boat moved faster and faster as the tidal wave came closer, and then, suddenly, there was no more wave. It merged back into the sky; indeed, had been the sky all the time. I tried to get out of the boat before it entered the garden, but the resin held me fast. I twisted and struggled, but the boat reentered the garden. I had to get out, because abruptly, I realized what lay beyond the icy wall that fenced in the far side of the garden. The boat moved faster, and I was held captive. The wall of ice loomed closer and closer, chilling every nerve in my body. I felt myself begin to scream as the boat entered the cavern through which the river left the garden. I suddenly realized that no world existed outside that wall.

I awoke with my body damp from sweat. The room was bright. I had slept through the night and probably would not have awakened for hours more had it not been for the strange dream. I got up from the bed (I had fallen asleep in the chair, but somehow I was in the bed) and went outside. The heat inside was stifling.

I walked with my head hung down, my hands shoved deep into my pockets. A tremendous fit of depression had overtaken me, the physical-mental result of overstimulation. I walked slowly and looked at the ugly houses on all sides of me. There were ugly clouds floating across an ugly sky; the sun shining down on an ugly earth. I thought back on my life and wondered how I had ever been happy with any of the asinine trivia I had ever attached importance to. My future looked equally dull and depressing. My mind was shut to beauty of any kind. I realized what was happening, but I could do nothing about it. It would be the same as expecting someone who is deliriously happy to try to see the dull side of things. It was a state of body as well as mind. My eyes began to itch furiously, and as I rubbed them, my nose began to run. I sniffled and my ears clogged up.

There is nothing that can be done for a depressive state except to ride it out, like a hangover. The best possible thing to do is to lock oneself up in a room and speak to no one. If I had not known the cause, the fit would have been nearly unbearable; such a state, misunderstood, often causes a multitude of self-destructive impulses.

I thought back on "the love scene," and it appeared in a pitiful, distorted light. It was impossible to squeeze a drop of beauty from anything. I went back to the room and took a few aspirin, determined to sleep if off, if possible. The Blind Prophet looked pityingly at me, but I wanted none of his pity . . . Even he looked as ugly as sin.

It was dark when I woke up again. I could hear a steady vibration near me. It took a minute for my faculties to become aware enough to recognize it as a snore. John lay spread-eagle on the far side of the immense bed. He had also been up for several days but, having done it often, was a master of the art. He knew how and when to sleep it off. I respected the sanctity of his repose and tried to return to mine, still not feeling very exuberant over the mere fact of being alive.

I almost succeeded until the chorus of "Apples, Peaches, and Cherries" started running through my mind for no apparent reason. Over and over it resounded as though through an echo chamber . . . "Crying apples, peaches, and cher-ries; apples, peaches and cher-ries . . . Rutabagas, soybeans, and Rach-maninoff . . . Persimmons, earthworms, and pum-pernickel . . ."

I was finally forced to accept the fact that my psyche was not about to drift into sweet slumber again. John continued to snore, and I decided to strangle him, but instead put on my jacket and went out.

I thought of walking to the bookstore, but it seemed like an incredibly distant objective . . . Coffeehouse? Maybe . . . My pockets were empty, though, and besides, there were bound to be people there . . . ugly, chattering people. Not so ugly as they might have seemed in the afternoon, but still not sufficiently alluring to make seeking them out worth the effort. I decided to go back to the room before I noticed that my undirected feet had carried me a good distance away. A fine mist was falling; not quite rain but gentle and soothing . . . infinitely to be preferred over John's contented snoring.

The street was iridescent with the sheen of oil from countless faulty crankcases, reflecting the prismatic colors from the too-bright streetlights that vainly persisted in their age-old battle with night.

I began to lift slowly from my depression. It was as though a tremendously heavy weight somewhere inside my head were being carried away by bits and pieces. I became mildly amused at the dependence the mind has upon the functions of the body. I could feel my consciousness almost as though it were a tangible thing . . . an immense nut, the core of which was a small kernel of awareness, protected (but blinded, as well) by a thick layer of shell.

A woman approached from the opposite direction, carrying a bag of groceries. The bag was softened by the mist, and the corner of a box of margarine protruded, showing steady promise, even as I watched, of enlarging its escape route for the benefit of the other denizens of the market.

I saw her face for a moment as we passed under a streetlight. I walked on a few steps, then had a sudden urge to run back and say something comforting to her, but my feet moved forward. Her face hung in my mind . . . It looked old but wasn't. She had looked as though she were crying, and her hair was a dull gray; her face loose with wrinkles and lines that were all wrong because they didn't seem to fit . . . a strange mixture between old age and a youth that seemed to cry out from behind the wrinkles . . . not a graceful old age but a youth that had suddenly been told that it was too ancient for pretty dresses and accepted the fact with great misgivings.

I stopped and looked back, but she had disappeared around a corner or somewhere into the darkness that seemed accentuated by tiers of streetlights vanishing into the distance, becoming a dull, uniform haze in the heavy mist. I turned again and looked ahead at a thousand more streetlights lying before me, then lit a cigarette and continued walking.

The night pressed down as though it were trying to drive me into the pavement. I began to wonder if everything was so pale as it suddenly seemed . . . ambition, the weight of potential silver in my pocket, the importance of my personal loves . . . The stream of cars, slowed to a crawl by the mist, seemed to merely drift by; each carrying phantom shapes, each phantom preoccupied with his ambitions, his wealth, his personal loves as he moved his car through what had become a gentle drizzle.

And to what can each cling, really, I wondered, *what would be his, separate and unique?* His loneliness, perhaps? And myself, was that my only claim to a uniqueness separating me from those phantom shapes? No . . . even that must be shared with uncounted others who had walked this highway at night with the gentle drizzle of rain in the air.

I tried to drag at my cigarette, but it had become sodden with rain. I threw it in the gutter, where the rain was already beginning to form small rivulets.

THERE OCCUR DAYS IN THE MOST PROSAIC LIVES UPON which nothing remarkable happens, and yet the day remains engraved on the memory just because it was remarkable in itself; "remarkable" because it was the very antithesis of "dying," in contrast to those days in which we find ourselves a little less alive than we had been the day before. These are the days that we give the catch-all tag of "memories," and they make the gathering of years a little less unpleasant because they happened. They touch the clouded mind softly and place a pleasant mist around accumulated years.

They are the days on which we really should have been doing something constructive but instead decided to do something with what we had already constructed, or perhaps happily forgot for a time that we *must* construct or ever have. These days sometimes occur while we are planning for our future and, for some reason, stop still in the midst of planning and begin to wonder . . . suddenly realizing that we were planning for *today* ten years ago (the idea of still planning, at this date, was not included in the plans) and may well spend the rest of our lives planning until suddenly there is no reason to plan anymore, because, inevitably, the rest has been preplanned *for* us. Realizing this is something akin to a short circuit, and there is no telling what unorthodox pleasures might be enjoyed before the system rectifies itself and reassumes normal functioning.

A child has little concern for his long-range future and so manages to live almost every day in a manner little short of mystical, until his mind is eventually corroded with concepts of security . . . the point at which he ceases to grow and begins the lifelong processes of decay. At this point, he is ripe to take his place among the masses who expend the flavor of their youths in consternation against the day when their fruit will begin to wither on the branch. And when it does, they worry about the day when the withered fruit will drop to the ground . . . and they are never disappointed, for it invariably *does* drop when the frosts pinch at the rotting stem.

BARBARA WANDERED INTO THE BOOKSTORE WEARING A PAIR OF short jeans, her hair tied into two nonchalantly bouncing ponytails. I was staring half consciously at the cover of a Swiss travel guide. It showed a small village at the base of the Alps, and I was trying to follow the main road of the village as it trailed off into the distance, encountering a stream on its way and several groves of trees. I was meeting with considerable success and could almost feel a cool wind blowing from the mountains as I mentally trudged along the road through the neat, white houses, past the steepled church, and into the valley.

"Well now, would you look at that!" Barbara said, scarcely able to conceal her contempt as she perched herself on a tabletop. Jerry was drumming on the back of his guitar, sitting in a beam of sunlight that poured in through the skylight. He looked bemused and vaguely dissatisfied, as though he knew he should be doing better things with the late-spring day. He looked up at Barbara and smiled detachedly, then closed his eyes and continued to drum.

"How can you people *sit* here on a day like this?" she asked, absolutely aghast.

"Hmm?" I replied, momentarily conveyed back from my trek through the Alps. Alan, who had been browsing through books on the other side of the store, came over. Barbara appealed to him: "How *can* you?"

"Well, I don't know," Alan replied, not having the faintest notion of whatever it might be she was beseeching of him, "but I've been managing for some time, off and on."

"Oh," she replied, drawing the word out to several syllables in obvious irritation. Alan was startled.

"Now, there. What's the trouble, Barb?"

"Oh, never mind, it's nothing . . . just nothing at all."

"That's good," Alan said, then turned to Jerry. "Have you seen this book on—"

"How can you all just sit here and do nothing on a day like this?" Barbara exploded. "You look like a bunch of slugs hiding under rocks."

Alan raised an eyebrow. "Well, what do you propose we should do instead?"

"Well . . ." She thought for a moment. Then, suddenly: "We have to have an *adventure*, and I know just the place to go."

I returned to Switzerland. An adventure sounded as though it would entail a much greater amount of physical energy than I felt able to muster. I'd almost reached the foot of the mountain when I was suddenly dragged back again from my excursion. It had been decided, in my absence, that I was to drive them up to a "castle" somewhere in the foothills.

"It's a *mar*velous place," Barbara assured us, and nothing would do but that we leave immediately.

After all . . . how could we just sit around on a day like this? Well . . .

Barbara and Alan scraped up fifty cents between them for gas money, enough to move the needle to the right side of the "Empty" mark, and we took off.

The rolling pastures through which the road sliced were peppered with cows going about cow business, ringing their bells and looking about as concerned over matters of importance as any other herd of cows on a spring afternoon. High, wispy clouds dabbled about the sky unbothered by much wind and seemed less aware of whatever might be passing beneath them than the cows were about what occurred around them. Jerry absently flipped a cigarette butt out of the window.

Alan looked mildly startled at the action. "Here, now . . . I don't want to disturb you, but I doubt if you realize the implications of what you just did."

"Huh?" Jerry replied blankly.

"Look out there, along the road." Alan pointed out with a furtive gesture. "Cigarette butts . . . millions of them. And that's only a small part of the *totality* of it all! Think of all the similar roads in the United States . . . Paris! . . . England! Streets all over the world, all strewn with cigarette butts thrown there by people like yourself, people unaware of the fact that they're sealing their *doom*! Someday those cigarette butts are going to become *aware*, and when they do, they're going to rise up and unite. From there, it's only a small step to world domination! Think of it, man: a world dominated by vast hordes of paranoid cigarette butts!"

"God, no . . ."

"Who knows what's going on, even now, in the warped filter of some Old Gold Hitler. I tell you, man . . . watch it before it's *too late*."

The words *paranoid cigarette butts* caught Alan's fancy, and he began to mumble them over and over. He tried setting melodies to the words and finally decided that Bach's "Little Fugue" had been deliberately constructed to fit the words: "See . . . the danger was even apparent to cultivated minds two hundred years ago. Farsighted as he was, Bach left a message to the future that only a blind fool could ignore . . ."

"Or discover," Jerry added.

Alan spent the rest of the journey to Barbara's castle conducting us in the singing of four-part inventions on the theme of paranoid cigarette butts.

"Here it is," Barbara said suddenly. I applied my brakes, pushing them to the floor, and we coasted about a hundred yards past the indicated spot.

"You could use a little brake fluid, maybe," Jerry observed.

"Brake fluid, hell. What I need is an anchor." We got out and commenced upon our adventure.

The gate to the "castle" was guarded by two stone lions who looked fierce in an abstract way and a worn sign that read No Trespassing, Violators Will Be Prosecuted. We proceeded with our violation by slipping through a hole in the surrounding fence, then started what proved to be a lengthy hike up a long, winding road.

The warm afternoon sun filtered through the trees, which interlaced their branches high overhead to force vast redwood canopies. The path curved up a gently ascending hill through pungently scented woods. The sunlight fell in rays where it broke through the mass of trees and bits of dust danced and glistened in them. Crickets chattered, blending in with the scenery in a sort of confused precision.

Jerry fastened a wreath out of what looked like poison oak branches and placed it on his head as he walked. Finishing the task, he began to strum his omnipresent guitar, playing soft melodies that drifted through the woods and seemed to hush all sound except our footsteps and the voices of a flock of invisible birds. A particular shade of green abounded everywhere, seeming to tint even the air, the color of green that is a blend of foliage, sunlight, and youth, a color once seen, never quite forgotten.

Jerry looked like some Pan, wreath and all, caught in his natural habitat, while meticulous Alan led the way up with a long stick in one hand, the other clasped around Barbara's.

We walked without saying anything for a while, each intricately involved in his own personal world. I felt as though I were following the yellow brick road and every bend in it seemed to uncover some new wonder: a fantastically shaped tree or a ray of sunlight falling suddenly in the middle of my path. I would not have been overly surprised to discover a tin woodsman rusting away for want of oil in his joints, in the deep creek bed that followed the road for a while before turning off to pursue its own devices . . . and the green . . . everywhere was the not-quite-tangible green.

Alan had advanced several yards before us, leaning on his stick. Suddenly, he stopped and turned, looking down the hill at us.

"Wait a minute," he commanded. Jerry continued to strum quietly. "This is how I want to remember you when I go back to England."

We stopped, etching him into our minds as he was etching us, as we were each lost for a moment in realization of our own beauty or whatever it was that made it so natural and quite in order that we should be on the road to the castle on this particular spring day in spite of No Trespassing signs and not-quite-ferocious lions.

The reverie was broken by the sound of a car engine. A few seconds later, a yellow convertible came around the corner from the direction in which we were heading. The car stopped. In it was a fat, bald man and an elderly woman with protruding lips and a ripple of chins, which oozed down her neck and disappeared under her collar. "Hey," the fat man snarled, "didn't you see the sign down there?" A gentle wind stirred his nasal hair as he spoke. We said nothing, and Jerry continued to strum softly.

"This is private property here, and we don't want you damned vandals running around messing things up, see?"

He cocked a bushy eyebrow, waiting for whatever smart comeback might be ventured. He could have waited until Christmas after next for all Jerry was concerned; a slight sneer that only someone well schooled in Jerry's facial expressions could have caught (or understood) rippled above his beard as he turned and started walking downhill.

"Yeah, and if we catch you around here again, you'll be seeing the police. Damned kids. Jesus!"

The fat man started his car again and continued on down. The mechanical grumble of his engine vanquished the magic green that had been our traveling companion thus far, sending it deep into the woods in bewildered haste.

Jerry turned around as soon as the car was out of earshot and started walking back up. Alan and Barbara followed.

"You know, maybe we'd better not . . . ," I said pensively. "He might be serious. We can always come back some other time." My illusion had been broken; something ugly had appeared in the midst of my green world . . . something akin to a sour note in a delicate violin passage.

"Hell," Jerry snorted and continued walking.

I started down the hill. The others walked on, not questioning my motivation, and I heard the guitar grow fainter and fainter until it disappeared, blending with the soft rustle of the trees as a cool wind played through them.

I came to the spot where Alan had told us to stop. I stood there for a minute, watching the dust forming varied spirals of color in a ray of errant sunlight that pierced through the trees to the ground. I kicked at a bank of moss that had formed over a rotting log, burying the toe of my shoe in the soft wood. A sizable bug scurried from under the log, carrying a white parcel that was no doubt of great value to him.

"How long have you been around here, and if so, why aren't you in jail, bug?" I queried him. He obviously didn't deem the question to be worthy of an answer for he continued about his business without so much as pausing to think it over. Suddenly, I obeyed my impulse to turn around and run back.

The running was exhilarating, and each time I rounded a corner, I felt lighter until I was out of breath and could run no more.

At the top of the hill were two roads. One was open, the other barred by a rusty chain. There was no doubt as to which one they had taken; the forbidden one, of course. I followed the road until suddenly, over a rise, the land flattened out, and the vista spread out before me for miles. The brilliant afternoon sky loomed over a tiny city crouched out in the distance, and the "castle" appeared abruptly in front of me.

It was not really a castle proper but something more on the line of a Spanish-style mansion in a state of singular disrepair, replete with many turrets and balconies. All things considered, however, it would do for a castle in a pinch.

As I approached the building, Alan suddenly appeared on the topmost terrace of the house. He spread his hands, orating to the world at large:

And death shall have no dominion,
Dead men naked, they shall be one
With the man and the wind and the west moon!

His voice echoed through the hollow mansion. Alan had a talent for doing the most ludicrous things in a manner little short of grandiose.

I entered through a side door. The huge living room looked as though it had been looted of everything except a large marble lion that seemed to have long ago fallen from a pedestal that was nowhere to be seen.

I walked through the living room and out to the veranda, which opened out over a sharply sloping hillside of ancient redwoods. The giant trees seemed to form a solid mass down the hill and into the distance, each raising a shabbily barbed spear toward the pale lapis lazuli sky, arching and beckoning as faint gusts of wind busied them.

Jerry sat on the cobbled steps staring over the trees while the sound of Alan's feet clattered loudly through the hush as he aided Barbara in exploring her castle.

He looked up at me for a second, then returned his gaze to the horizon, which loomed over the trees. "Decided to come?" he asked with a faint smile.

"Yes."

I T WAS A VERY LONG ROAD THAT SEEMED TO STRETCH INTO infinity. There was no moon in the sky, and yet a kind of moonlight poured onto the road, glinting from the scarlet stones that crushed into powder as I stepped on them. I wondered how long I had been walking, and I looked at my watch. It said, in italic print, that I had been walking for about twenty years and requested that it be wound. I tried to wind it but could find no stem with which to do so. I decided to take it to a watchmaker if I happened to see one along the road.

The road was lined with trees. They were ancient and gnarled, shimmering with a pale white phosphorescence in the moonlike light. A large black bird swooped over the trees, and one of the branches darted up and snatched it. The bird screamed, a loud, piercing human scream.

The scream seemed to take form as it left the bird's throat and began to circle aimlessly in the pale light until the trees, finished with the bird, leisurely twined their limbs into a net and snared it, dragging it down into their slathering mass.

I felt a hot pain in my heel and started to run. The trees noticed me suddenly, and a network of grasping branches snaked out to stop me. As soon as I was out of their reach, one of the trees, the nearest to me, began to moan in a shrill voice. I stopped, a comfortable distance away, and looked back.

The tree held up a cigarette, tightly clasped in its leafless claw, promising loudly that I could have it if I would submit to being eaten. Its voice sounded somewhat like the noise made when scratching a bow across the strings of a violin, behind the bridge.

Another tree held up an eggbeater, with the same stipulation. I turned from the ludicrous scene and began running again.

Suddenly, it started to rain. The rain fell in crimson drops that became paving stones as soon as they hit the road. I started to run faster, hoping to find some sort of shelter from the onslaught. Several of the trees uprooted themselves and came running after me, waving cigarettes and eggbeaters and insurance policies, screaming, "All you have to do is let us eat you. We may not give you another chance, you know!"

I ran into a store that appeared beside the road. There was a large sign outside that read WATCHMAKER. My watch started to buzz as soon as I saw the sign. I slammed the glass front door and threw the heavy wooden latch into place. The trees, which had been closer to catching me than I thought, lined up against the display window and began to tap on the glass. A voice behind me suddenly said, "What can I do for you, Mau-Mau?"

"What?" I answered, spinning around to discover the source of the voice. "Who said that? I'm not a Mau-Mau, whoever you are."

"Then why aren't you wearing shoes?" the voice replied. It belonged to a midget who became visible as he hopped up on a chair behind the counter.

I ignored the question, instead taking my watch off. "Can you fix this for me?"

"Let me see your Social Security card first," he replied in a nasty tone.

I looked for my wallet, then realized that I was naked. I began to clasp and unclasp my hands in bewilderment. A tree tapped on the window and held up a Social Security card, pointing at his mouth with another branch.

"No!" I shouted.

The midget suddenly became interested in my watch. He picked it up and began to examine it carefully. He looked over each detail, shook it, then placed it to his ear. Finally, he asked, "Leather soles or rubber?"

"Neither. I just want my watch fixed."

He shook his head sadly from side to side. "Then what are you doing in a shoe store?"

"But the sign outside says that you're a watchmaker."

"I just put that up to fool the Mau-Maus. They don't generally carry watches . . . unless they *steal* them," he added, looking suspiciously at me. "Now then, what flavor of shoestrings do you prefer?"

"I don't want anything to *do* with shoes, damn it. I just want to get my watch fixed."

"In that case, I guess I can't help you. You Mau-Maus are all alike. Bad for business. Go on home and eat dinner." He hopped off the stool and disappeared. I turned to the window. The trees were still waiting outside.

"Wait," I said. The midget lifted his large head above the counter suspiciously. "I'll have some shoes after all. I can't go outside."

"Too late. We're closed now." He lifted a heavy rock from behind the counter on which was written the word CLOSED in crude red letters. Then he put the rock back under the counter. "Run along

147

like a good Mau-Mau," he said, "and shut off the lights when you leave."

I picked up a knife that was lying on the counter. "Don't make me go!" I hollered, waving the knife at him.

He smiled and shook his head. "You Mau-Maus are all alike." He left the room. The lights switched off, leaving the shop in darkness. All I could see were the trees, lined up outside the window waving their cigarettes and eggbeaters. The midget came back with a gun.

"Now go," he said, "and be sure you don't steal anything on the way out." I noticed my watch hanging around his neck, suspended by a shoestring.

"Give me my watch back first," I said.

"Nonsense. It wasn't your watch in the first place." My watch leered at me from its place around the midget's neck, as though it agreed with him.

"Mau-Mau," the watch said maliciously.

"Damn it, I won't leave until you give it back!" I shouted furiously.

The shopkeeper drew himself up to his full height. He seemed to grow until his head touched the ceiling. "Mau-Mau!" he shrieked at me, and the words echoed from the corners of the darkened room, repeating themselves over and over in a mounting cascade of accusation.

I turned and ran for the door. The trees outside took up the chorus of "Mau-Mau, Mau-Mau" and threw their eggbeaters and insurance policies against the window in a frenzy. The walls of the room started to buckle together, forcing me toward the door. I ran back to the counter, but the door suddenly broke open and the trees began to swarm through. The store disappeared entirely, and I found myself abruptly back on the road.

The road was lined with the trees, each holding some worthless piece of trash to charm me with. They seemed to have re-rooted while I was in the shop and were thrashing about trying to uproot again.

My heart was beating furiously, and I could taste blood in my mouth as I ran beneath the looming, steel-gray sky. The rain was still falling, and the road was hopelessly slick. I stumbled and fell, and as I did, I suddenly realized that the road was moving backward, back toward the trees.

I was completely exhausted and could not get up again, even though I could feel myself being drawn back.

The air was suddenly split by a shrill trumpet blast. Upon hearing this, the trees set up a wailing and chanting chorus. The bloodred rain turned into hailstones, each one screaming in agony as it hit the ground. I suddenly realized that I was screaming along with them and that blood was pouring from my mouth, spilling out and forming shimmering puddles on the road.

The trumpet shrilled again and an elevator crashed down from the sky, landing next to me in a pool of blood and rain. The door slid open as soon as it hit, and a voice from within cried, "All aboard for Venezuela!"

I began to crawl toward the door, a sudden vision of hope flooding over me. A bright light flashed out and searched up and down me, then it flicked off.

"Sorry," the voice echoed as though originating from deep within a tunnel, "we can't take any Mau-Maus on this run."

"But I'm not a Mau-Mau!" I screamed at the voice. The door slid shut on further argument, and the elevator shot quickly back out of sight into the dull gray sky.

The trees continued to wait and thrash, waving their valueless considerations. I slumped down on the road, feeling myself being borne helplessly toward them.

THERE WAS NO ONE IN THE ROOM WHEN I AWOKE. I GOT UP AND searched for the light switch. I searched for quite a while before I remembered that there *was* no light switch and pulled the light cord instead.

There was an acrid smell in the room. I looked for the source of it and discovered a cigarette butt smoldering in a wax cup. A recording of "Daphnis and Chloé" was spinning idly on the turntable of the phonograph going, "Ish, ish, ish," as the arm played the final groove over and over.

A partially ravished can of pears sat on the table, collecting various and sundry insects, which I brushed away before consuming the rest of the can. Eating them was a mistake, for I suddenly realized that I was hungry. I tried to sublimate by prowling through the numerous cigarette-butt depositories, unsuccessfully, for any goodly remnants. Someone had obviously been there first. I was reduced to picking out a few butts, none exceeding an eighth of an inch in length, shredding them, and piling the bits of tobacco in a heap until I had collected enough nicotine-sodden grains to roll a satisfactory cigarette. I lit it and took a puff, then put it down in a puddle of pear juice, which suddenly and maliciously appeared out of nowhere. I cursed half-heartedly, decided that I didn't want the cigarette anyway, put on my jacket, and exited.

"Where you going?" I asked myself curiously as I descended the stairs.

"Hell if *I* know."

"How you going to get there?"

"Fastest way possible. Why?"

"Just curious. Have fun."

It was a warm evening. I took off my coat and slung it over my shoulder as I walked along. I began to feel somewhat picturesque. A good-sized cigarette butt lay beside the road, but I walked jauntily by it, feeling too proud to bend over and pick it up.

I had a short battle between my conscience and my cigarette habit, swallowed my pride, retraced my steps, and picked it up.

As I walked, I had a sudden vision of a baked potato, crisply done and oozing with butter. The imaginary potato loomed in the air just in front of me. I tried vainly to push the illusion out of my mind. No doubt about it, I was *damnably* hungry. I began to feel slightly dizzy, and my feet were progressing, one in front of the other, with no conscious direction on my part.

"Decided where you're going yet?" I asked myself.

"No, damn it. Go away."

"How?"

I suddenly decided that I didn't really want the potato. My stomach was beginning to feel tight and giddy. I felt as though I had been walking for hours.

"Don't you think we ought to sit down and rest for a while?"

"No, we might freeze to death."

"Not if we buy a parachute to keep warm with. I hear you can get a good silk parachute rather cheaply at a surplus store."

"Who's got the money to buy a parachute? If I didn't know better, I'd say you were going off your nut!"

The sky was a deep bluish black; it seemed to be some sort of monstrous inverted bowl. I had a sudden feeling that I was in a room of infinite proportions.

Meanwhile, my feet directed me in a pattern they had become used to, and I ended up sitting at a table in the bookstore.

Jerry was sitting at the table, blitheringly inanely at Grace Marie. I suddenly realized that I had come to some place as I awoke from the semi-hypnotic daze in which I had been wandering.

I watched them with a dull stare, half listening to their conversation and half thinking what a wondrous physical sensation it would be to have one's bladder filled so tightly it seemed ready to burst, and then to urinate for an hour, feeling the tenseness leaving one's body until there was complete peace . . . then to try to do the same thing mentally (in a manner of speaking).

Jerry was enlightening Grace Marie as to his various methods of seduction and other topics dear to his heart.

"You know, I don't like the guys who come up with 'It's good for your complexion' or 'If you don't do it, you're socially maladjusted, my dear,'" Grace was commenting. "I like men with more positive attitudes . . . like 'I'm ready if you are, bitch, and if you aren't, you'd damn well better think about it quick' or something on that line. There's too damned many guys that're always trying to hustle a poor girl with those moth-eaten psychological lines. It's positively insidious."

"The only trouble with being insidious," Jerry answered, stroking his beard insidiously, "is that it takes too much time to get the same thing you get by being to the point. Now me, I've got it down to a science of a sort. My formula is: sing, smile, and nod. Works damned near every time. I feel somewhat like a hawk when I'm on the prowl. I just sort of hover over the chicken coop until I see a nice fat one, then . . . swoop!" He made a gesture in the air to accompany his dialectic. "It's my studied conviction that they're there for me, so why not make use of them?"

"Very good, my dear. I wish there were more with your turn of mind. It gets pretty maddening sometimes, watching some idiot blunder around telling you how soulful your eyes are or how silky your hair is.

"Hell, I've been living with my goddamned hair for over twenty-five years, and it's just as stringy as it ever was. It gets so that a poor girl almost has to rape them to shut them up!"

The perpetual music that drifted through the store stopped, and the announcer said something about "Save and grow with the Bank of America."

"What'd he say?" Grace Marie asked, startled. "Save and groove with the Bank of America?"

"Yeah," Jerry laughed. "Swing while you save."

"Banks aren't supposed to be like that. They're supposed to be impressive and secure."

"They're probably trying to get rid of that image. Probably scares too many people away. 'Swing to the poorhouse with us; we are *not* a bum-kick bank!'"

They chattered on endlessly, improvising on the theme. My head began to ache. I excused myself and went into the bathroom, where I tried to answer the demands of my stomach by drinking voluminous quantities of tap water.

As I left the bathroom, a picture flashed through my mind of an endless succession of days such as this, past and future. I began to wonder just what in hell I was doing here, sitting in the bookstore with the waiting and the hunger. I went to another table and sat down, cradling my head in my arms as the headache continued.

Something suddenly felt terribly wrong. I could hear Jerry and Grace Marie chattering on and on, and I wished to God that they'd stop. I felt nauseous, partially from hunger and partially from the realization that I had fallen into a pattern, the very thing I pretended to despise. It came to me with an ever-increasing flood of dismay that I was living a very-well-ordered pattern of "bohemian" existence . . . almost a *security* in my insecurity.

Unpleasant thoughts ran through my mind, one on the tail of another. I began to wonder if perhaps we weren't a bedraggled pack of screwed-up people, watching and hating the world of purpose and security through screwed-up eyes.

The walls were beginning to close in subtly, and still I waited. I began to question this word *waiting*. Was I waiting or postponing, and why? Why, why, why?

The walls were coming closer as I waited for them to expand. I began to wonder, almost bitterly, if perhaps that for which I waited was not in some dark corner somewhere waiting for *me*.

I suddenly tore myself away from the table and left the bookstore. I began to dazedly retrace my steps back to the room.

Suddenly, I realized that I was walking along a very narrow road that seemed to stretch to infinity . . . and I half expected the trees to begin uprooting themselves.

IT WAS APPROACHING MIDNIGHT, AND THE MUSIC WAS BECOM-ing unbearably monotonous. We were sitting in Marty's apartment while a five-piece bluegrass band practiced. The skillful, though overpowering, twang of the Scruggs-style banjo, reinforced by two dreadnought guitars, a mandolin, and a bass constructed out of a broom handle, a bass string, and a metal washtub, was becoming unnerving.

John sat in the dimly lit room staring half consciously into space. His head nodded languidly to the music, unable to totally shut out the driving beat of note after note that cascaded from the combined instruments.

Jackson, jazz trumpet player of the "Jackson School" (a unique, unrecognized form) had long ago "split the scene," largely untainted by "that hillbilly jazz," and was presumably pedaling his bicycle aimlessly through the streets, looking for his mind.

Alan, alone, seemed to be impermeable, sitting with his note-book open, writing leisurely, occasionally stopping to run his hand through his hair or chew his eraser in momentary consternation. I looked half curiously over his shoulder: "In the beginning was insanity and the primordial writhing was the void . . ." Well, so much for that. I sat back and watched Jerry. He stood, one leg perched on a footstool, with a look of intense admiration for the agile sounds that issued forth:

Standin' on the corner with the low down blues,
A great big hole in the bottom of my shoes,
Honey, let me be your Salty Dowg [dog],
Lemme be your Salty Dowg,
Or I won't be yer man at all,
Honey, let me be your Salty Dowg
(bum-scratch-bum-twang-bum-a-ditty-twang . . .)

John turned to me after a particularly intricate banjo break-down. "Let's make it somewhere, man."

"Where to?"

"I dunno, but this stuff's driving me out of my gourd. Let's go get some coffee."

"The place closes in half an hour. A quarter is a lot to spend just to sit there that long."

"Well, hell, don't buy anything, then."

"They've got a new policy to discourage customers . . . You've got to buy something to sit there."

"Hell, I'll treat if you're that down-and-out; let's make it before I turn into a puddle and stain the furniture."

"Sure. Where's my jacket?"

"You're sitting on it."

We left the apartment and headed for the coffeehouse. We walked half the way in silence until John suddenly said, "Can you feature some cats spending their *lives* doing that?" He shook his head and shoved his hands into the pockets of his beat-up leather jacket. I buttoned my shirt at the neck, being ill protected by my ancient zipperless jacket. The air had a clean, cold nip to it. Summer was well over, and the nights were becoming progressively chillier.

With a squeaking overture of unoiled wheels, Jackson suddenly appeared around a corner, pedaling leisurely. He was wearing his omnipresent green fedora and trumpet, which hung loosely from the handlebars, tied in the pillowcase he generally carried it in (Jackson's trumpet was an article of clothing more necessary to him than pants).

"Hiya, Jacks," John said without great enthusiasm.

"Salutations. May I ask, 'Quo vadis?' or, in a word, whitherfore art thou headed?" Jackson spoke softly and emphatically in the language that was characteristic of the Jackson School, the school of unrequited love and misunderstood music.

"Coffeehouse. You coming?"

"M." (This word he pronounced with a great deal of conviction, emitting it from the depths of his soul like the spiritual-mystic "Om," but signifying, generally, a complete and utter impotence in the face of universal insanity.) "I find myself in the gutter without butter or, in a word, lacking of due funds with which to procure any dainties at aforementioned establishment. However, should you find it in—"

"I'm almost busted, man. I'm already taking Bob here on a free ride," John said, anticipating the forthcoming question.

"In that case, I shall tear myself away from your delightful companionship and continue my quest for the Holy Grail. Mayhap this very eve I shall chance upon some kindly philanthropist who will deem it consummate joy to accompany mineself to the liquor store to procure for ourselves some peppermint schnapps or like goodies. M." Jackson pedaled away, his round, dark figure seated proudly upon the bicycle, continuing his lifelong quest for an appreciative audience and good spirits.

We entered the coffeehouse and sat down near the window. John wrapped his lank frame around a chair and commenced to gaze at the wall after tilting his limp army fatigue cap—he called it his "soul hat"—back on his head. It had been my fatigue cap once, but John had appropriated it, claiming that his soul was intimately related to it and that it would be a sin of nigh Gargantuan proportion to demand its return. What could I do except let the fatigue cap join John's leather jacket and marvelous car as the outward manifestations of his inner being?

We sat silently for a while, the monotony of Marty's replaced by the monotony of the coffeehouse; the monotony of the bluegrass band replaced by the monotony of whatever unremarkable music issued from the FM "good music" station omnipresent in the coffeehouse.

"So what's on your mind, John?"

"I dunno, man, I dunno. I'm just wondering what in hell this is all about."

"Nothing like starting out with culminating questions."

"Complex, hmm? I don't know. Maybe it's just so damned uncomplex I can't see it. Forest-for-the-trees bit, you know. Anyway, I'm not just 'starting out' like you said"—he tapped his fingers nervously on the table—"it's been on my mind for a hell of a long time. Sometimes I can forget it . . . that's what the scene does for me . . . but then I feel guilty about wasting time later." He looked over at the waiter, but the waiter seemed to feel like taking his own good time to get around to us and was engaged in folding napkins. "For going on to four years now, it's been one scene after another, and sometimes I think I'm hooked, man. Every once in a while, I realize that the only thing I'm living for is the scene, and that scares me, so I come up with something like that damned commune idea and kid myself around that I'm accomplishing something. What's it all for, man? That's what I have to find out. I've got to find it out before I decide that it's all about nothing . . . no reason at all . . . and blow my brains out or hit the needle."

"Don't feel like the Lone Ranger, fella. A lot of people run around and say they know and try to tell you all about it . . . and maybe it works for them . . . self-hypnosis or something . . . but I doubt if they do. They find their cog in the wheel and think it's God, then go around preaching it and making people who *know* they don't know feel like maybe there really *is* a reason. And when they can't find it . . . and everyone else seems to be finding it and being happy about the whole thing, they start feeling like you do. I think if you really *did* know the score, you could tell God to step aside.

"The first time you showed your face around here, you asked me what the score was, and I gave you some half-assed answer or other . . . and maybe it was the *right* answer. Maybe it's just something you do until you can't anymore, and then you don't."

John looked puzzled and pulled his cap down to his forehead. He caught the rhythm of the FM music and nodded his head unconsciously to it. He began to speak very slowly in contrast to his usual rapid-fire conversation. "You know, man, I've gotten to the point where I don't *give* a good goddamn about *why*. Seriously, that's my way of thinking now. I don't go around asking, 'Why?' but that's the only answer I get. I don't come up to you or anybody and ask, 'Why the scene?' I want to know, '*What's* the scene?' Philosophers and psychiatrists are all wrapped up in 'whys.' What I want to know is *what*. *What* in hell am I supposed to be doing here." He pushed the cap back to its former position and looked past me at the wall. A humorless smile played unconsciously across the seldom-relaxed features of his sharply angled face. I didn't answer. A few epigrammatical thoughts flickered through my mind, but none of them answered the question posed, and besides, I wasn't in the mood to play either Ben Franklin or Oscar Wilde. It didn't seem quite in character, somehow, for John "the Cool," as we tagged him, to be questioning the values of being, and I began subconsciously to rearrange my evaluation of him.

"Jesus, John, I never figured you had things like this going for you."

"I don't broadcast very often; that's not my scene. Besides"—he laughed without humor—"it doesn't fit the image. Know what I mean?"

"I think so."

"You know who I am? I'm 'John the Cool.' Species *Johnus coolus* or some such crap. That's the way it goes around here . . . you're not really a person; you're the label it's handy to tack on to you. You write sometimes, so you're 'Bob the Writer'; Jerry plays guitar, so he's 'Jerry the Guitar Player.' Then there's 'Alan the Poet' and 'Fred the Pill Head' . . . I can just picture Jerry coming to a party some night without a guitar: 'Hey, man, where's your axe?' 'I didn't bring it. Don't feel like playing.' 'Are you serious, man? What's wrong with you?' 'My mother just died.' 'Well, maybe we can dig up a guitar somewhere and you can play funeral dirges.' Get the scene?"

"Yeah, I guess I do. I hadn't thought about it like that . . . but I guess I do."

"You know this organizing bit everyone's tacked onto me? No one really bothers to dig much deeper . . . I'm John the Cool, and

I organize. Well, hell *yes*, I organize things; I always feel if I don't do it, nothing will ever happen. I go overboard sometimes, but I've got to keep my hand in something."

"Why? It ran more or less the same way before you ever appeared."

He seemed taken slightly aback, then nodded. "I'm hip to that. There isn't any reason for ninety percent of it, but, man . . . I've *got* to do something."

He stared at the fascinating point on the wall again. His face was too taut to wrinkle in a frown, but the haunted look that emanated from his unfocusing eyes was eloquent enough.

"That's why you keep hitting the road, John?"

"Yeah . . . I guess . . . I dunno. Maybe. You know how they say your feet get to itch? They do, man. I've woken up in the middle of the night at home feeling that way, and before the sun comes up, I'm halfway to LA."

He took a packet of cigarette papers from his jacket pocket and poked in the ashtray for butts. Finding a few, he shredded them and rolled the captured remains of tobacco into a cigarette and lit it.

"I mean to tell you, it gets *cold* in them boxcars, but at least I feel like I'm heading for something. It's never there, though, and sometimes I'll suddenly find myself a thousand miles away from home, and I wonder what in hell I'm doing and if I look any different from the rest of 'bos riding the rattlers.

"It's a bad scene, man." He shook his head. "Never let it get a hold of you. It's a *hard* lady to shake, I mean to tell you."

"I don't know . . . I'd like to give it a try, just so I can say I've done it. If I'd had half of your experiences, I'd write two books a day to tell about it."

"Be pretty dull after the first one. It's not that so many things happen . . . they do, but it's the anticipation of what you *might* do that makes you go in the first place. You think you'd learn after the first couple of trips. Uh-uh, you don't; you just gotta believe what the rest of the bums tell you and jump off that freight while you've still got some place to jump to. They found out the hard way, and they'll tell you, but it doesn't do them any good to know; they're stuck with it, and that's all she wrote."

A wistful half smile curled his mouth. "You can always shake a habit the first couple of times, but don't let it get too far or it'll shake you. Hey, you got a real cigarette on you?"

"Yeah, I borrowed a couple at the party."

He took one and crushed out his handmade cigarette with a look of distaste. The waiter came to the table and spread out two menus.

"Well, let's see," John said, studying the menu he probably knew by heart. "Can we make it by on one regular coffee?" he queried.

"Sorry, sir. You'll both have to order something if you sit here."

"All right. Two regular," he said, waving the waiter away with an aristocratic flick of his hand. When the coffee came, he drank his down quickly.

"I didn't want the damned stuff, but I shelled out good money for it, so by God, I'll drink it . . . and a couple of refills too."

After polishing off the cup and signaling for a refill, he settled back onto the chair. "So"—he shrugged lightly—"what's a man supposed to do?"

"Why not take up something? Ever thought of blowing a horn?" I knew that the comment was superfluous as soon as it left my tongue.

164

He looked slightly annoyed. "Or maybe stamp collecting? I wouldn't care if I had the potential to blow like Coltrane; that's not what I want."

"Do you have the vaguest idea of what you *do* want?"

"That I know . . . I want to do something that'll last. I want power; I want to be able to make things run." He said this with no trace of excitement in his voice. Undue emotion was, to him, the prime betrayer . . . not to be called upon except when the situation demanded (and rarely then). To do so would be a loss of "coolness," and that was unheard of.

He spread his hands on the table: thin hands, long and tapered as those of an artist should be, but with no desire to stroke a keyboard or guide a brush; impotent hands, but hands that could riff a deck of cards with consummate skill; hands trained in the toss of the percentage dice and the bottom deal in order to fill an empty stomach on a long, foreign road. "And that's the way the cards fall, man. Five-card no-peek."

"*Mais la joux ce ne fait pas* yet; at least not until you turn the cards over. It's too bad there's no art form where a man can stand up and say, 'I am,' and it could be appreciated without him having to paint or write about it, but there isn't. Your big trouble is that you have so much to say and no way to go about saying it. The most directionless person in the world is probably an artist without an art. He just doesn't . . ."

"Hold it. You don't have to draw me a diagram of my cross; I've been carrying it long enough to recognize it."

"Sorry, I didn't mean to expound . . . I . . . Well, hell, I did mean to."

"All right." He leaned back, tilting his chair against the wall, and dragged at his cigarette, then pointed a finger at me. "You know what makes this world run? It's the people who want to *make* something. Most of the people I know won't ever amount to anything, and they could give a hell less. They don't care if there's a statue of them in the park for the pigeons to drop their loads on or not. All they worry about is getting an old lady to have their kids for them. Hell's bells, this world doesn't need any more kids; it needs to do something with the ones it's got. You ask one of the little 'mothers' what in hell it's all about, and he doesn't know whether to shit or go blind. All he wants to do is grow up, smoke his goddamned cigarettes, and raise more kids. I'd just as soon stop now if I thought I'd end up like that."

"Okay, so you don't end up like that, and some kid five hundred years from now knows your name and birthday . . . maybe even gets out of school for it. What's this going to net you? What in the hell difference does it make?"

"I already told you I don't give a damn about why. I'll worry about that when I find *what*. Hell, you want to go back to the party? Looks like they're ready to lock up here."

My desire to return was mild, but there was no place else to go.

The music was still going strong. I sat down on the sofa and concentrated on the banjo player, waiting for him to screw up a break or lose a string, while the "gut-bucket bass" went *thump-thump-thump* like an abnormal pulse.

"Can you feature some cats spending their *lives* doing that?" John had said. Why not? I closed my eyes and tried to doze.

NO SOONER HAD I CLOSED MY EYES, IT SEEMED, THAN I opened them to find myself again enmeshed in sounds and one night had faded, like a movie shot, into the next. I tried, vainly, to recall what had happened during the day . . . then realized that it had never existed. As the realization rang through my mind, I sat my wineglass down and tried to get my bearings. They refused to come, and the very idea of assimilating them was insidiously shattered by two blaring saxophones, screaming up and down the chromatic scale in search of jazz. A half dozen people were pounding on conga drums, bongos, and the backs of chairs with varying frantic beats. An electric guitar set the pace, and Jackson, his trumpet in a pawnshop, was working out on an upright E-flat alto horn, completely and blissfully oblivious to whatever beat and tempo the music had. He occasionally took the horn from his lips to wipe the sweat from his forehead and empty his gurgling spit valves, then would launch back into the melee, notes akimbo.

I sat heavily on a chair and pushed it back against the wall, teetering on two legs. Every few seconds, the music would seem to disappear as stray thoughts tried to force themselves to the surface of my mind. They would almost succeed until a shattering, discordant blast from Jackson's horn forced them back into the depths and perspective would suddenly blare back into the fore.

I closed my eyes tightly, but the forms about me refused to vanish and continued stumbling and dancing across the panoramic screen of my eyelids.

"Hi, Bob; how's it going?" I snapped open my eyes and perceived an idiotic, drunken grin, nodded with a mechanical smile, and shut them again.

"Hey, Bob," the voice persisted. "You sure look bum-kicked. Have a drink and enjoy yourself. C'mon!"

"No, I'm tired. Go away." The voice said something incomprehensible and moved on.

I suddenly realized that I was terrified, but forced the concept back as suddenly as it had manifested itself. It was replaced by apprehension as I began to wonder, somewhat confusedly, what was wrong. A few months ago, I would have enjoyed holy hell out of such a party, but now all I could do was to sit back and feel helpless. I opened my eyes and let them wander haphazardly across the room. A rather ordinarily pretty blond girl was sitting across the room from me. Our eyes met, then slid away. I toyed idly with the idea of going over and striking up a conversation, but ennui held me fast to the chair while my mind drifted to other parts of the room.

I forced myself up from the chair and walked down the hall, threading my way through congealed clots of people until I found the bathroom. I closed the door and turned off the light, then lit a cigarette. I stared at the burning ember, half hearing the music that drifted in from the other room. It suddenly sounded as though it were miles away and not quite real. Suddenly, someone was pounding on the door, demanding entry. I turned on the light and flushed the toilet, a useless token to explain my presence in the room. The banging on the door grew insistent, but I felt incapable of moving from my momentary haven. I caught my reflection in the mirror above the sink and began to study it, not quite sure that the pale, green-tinged face that stared back was my own. I made a sudden face at it, then opened the door. The person who had been beating had mysteriously disappeared.

The muffled sound of a guitar issued from behind a closed door across from the bathroom. I opened the door and looked in. Jerry sat there by himself, picking idly at his instrument. I stood there for a moment, not quite sure if I should say anything or just go about my business. He didn't look up. His eyes were fixed hollowly on a point on the floor, and an inch-long ash had formed on the cigarette that smoldered in the tray at his feet. I closed the door and worked my way back up the hall, bits of unconnected thoughts and emotions running through my mind. It was odd . . . there was Jerry . . . the focal point of an almost infinite number of radii around which the "scene" revolved, by himself . . . unheeded. Strange, and yet it would be strange if he were not there. He was still Jerry, at least physically, and yet something was missing . . . or something new had been added, and he sat alone in a room.

Jerry: whom he loved was loved, whom he hated was despised; whosoever's sins he remitted, they were remitted . . . alone, picking on his guitar.

I went into the kitchen and poured some wine into a soda bottle, for want of glasses, tasted it, running the vinegar-like vintage around my tongue, then set it down for whomever might be more in the mood to appreciate it. A sax player came into the kitchen and asked who that bottle of wine belonged to.

"You can have it," I said, then, for want of something better to say, "I've had too much already."

"Why, thanks, man. I appreciate it. Say, this is some scene, hmm?"

"Yeah. You're really blowing a wicked sax there," I answered, suddenly feeling as though I were clutching at straws to keep from falling headlong into whatever the chasm below held.

"Why, thanks, man. Me and my axe here are a single soul tonight. Hee hee." He upended the bottle and chugged the wine down in one breath, then staggered back into the living room to add to the infernal racket.

"Hey, Bob. You look bum-kicked. Why don't you get in and enjoy yourself?"

"Hi, Karen. I'm *having* a good time," I answered. I felt as though my right to exist had suddenly been challenged. "I'm just on a solitary kick . . . digging people."

She looked at me with a half smile, and I felt guilty that I wasn't enjoying myself. But *damn it*, what was it to her? Why was she so concerned about me having a good time?

"Sorry," I laughed. "Guess I *am* bum-kicked. Hell, you can't enjoy yourself all the time."

"You don't have to apologize to me; I'm not in charge here." She pressed my hand and winked, then disappeared into the melee with her cup of bad wine.

Jerry came into the kitchen, his coat slung over his shoulder, and stood there a minute as though at a loss for something.

"Going home?" I asked.

"Guess so."

"Got a ride?"

"No. I think I'll walk."

"Mm. Want company?"

"Sure," he answered without enthusiasm. "I guess so."

I extricated my jacket from under a set of preoccupied lovers and borrowed some cigarettes from Grace Marie, so as not to expire of a nicotine fit on the long walk back to the room.

We skipped polite goodbyes and left the house. A cool wind blew open the zipperless flaps of my jacket, cleansing away the lingering scent of smoke and perspiration that filled the house. We walked on in silence for a while.

"Quite a party," I said, finally, for want of something better. I wanted to talk . . . Jerry knew something that I knew and I knew something that he did, but the only way to find out what it was, was by talking. Feelings are often devoid of intelligence, and one must rationalize them out by conversation, sometimes, in order to feel justified in having them.

"I didn't notice much. I'm getting sick and tired of them night after night. Don't know why I keep going . . . I don't know what it is, Bob, but I'm beginning to feel so damned uneasy." Suddenly, it was coming out; all that he had needed was the excuse, or we might have walked the five miles in silence. "I figured that I knew what the trouble was last month; that's why I got the job at the music store. I thought the reason for all this damned depression and aimlessness was because of being broke and not knowing where my next meal was coming from. Now that I've got a little money, I've got to face facts; it's not money . . . it's me. Whatever it was is still wrong, only I don't have anything concrete like not eating to pin it on now, and it's driving me nuts. I don't know if

I'm growing up or down, but I'm becoming a different person. It's weird, man, I meant to tell you."

I thought of a dozen answers as he talked but couldn't remember any of them by the time he had finished. We walked a little farther in silence, a flood of thoughts running through my mind. As I conceived them, I seemed almost to be saying them, and I could feel the silent replies from Jerry's mind.

A motor scooter suddenly rounded the corner bearing "Mad John" and Laird. "Hey, you guys splitting?" Laird hollered.

"The party's just starting," Mad John echoed. "Have a potato chip . . . Hell, have two!" He held out a bag, and I took the specified number.

"Getting tired. Too much partying," Jerry said.

"Well, later for ya, then," and the motor scooter sped off.

"Great guys, huh?"

"That's the trouble around here," Jerry replied earnestly, "too damned many great people. I sometimes feel like I should make it off somewhere, but I know I'll keep coming back. Everything I want is here, I guess . . . probably anywhere, for that matter. There's just that old problem of finding out just what in hell it is I *do* want."

"I don't know if I agree . . . at least in my case. The scene's changed a lot since I first latched on. Seems like it's top-heavy with the stock emotionally disturbed adolescent type . . . I had enough trouble with my own without nursing their neurosi too."

"Or maybe it's been like that all along . . . 'forest for the trees' and like that."

"Could be, but somehow I'd prefer not to think of it like that. It was too good while it lasted; no sense in spoiling the aftertaste."

We crossed the overpass that spanned the freeway. The highway stretched under the bridge, a ribbon of ceaselessly moving lights, into San Francisco. We stopped and looked down on the traffic.

"It's amazing there aren't more crack-ups than there are at the speed those people are going. I wonder where they're off to in such a rush."

"Or if the world would be changed much if one of them never got there," I added, irreverently flicking the remains of a cigarette down onto the dazzling stream of vanishing taillights and oncoming beams. The butt just missed the back of a small truck and hit the highway, spewing out a miniature universe of dying red suns. The truck vanished, blending in with a thousand other red taillights, never to know that I existed . . . or had added to the infinite number of actions occurring in the universe by flicking my cigarette butt onto the highway.

Jerry laughed. "You know, for a minute, I felt as though I were in charge here and could direct any one of these people's fates like moving a pawn!"

"You could, if you had enough large rocks to drop on them."

"Or thunderbolts."

We started walking again. "None of us has any trouble destroying things," I observed. "What's rarer is someone who can create things as well."

"You sound like somebody's philosophy teacher."

"No, seriously . . . Have you ever created anything? I don't mean just splashing paint on a canvas, I mean like really make something out of nothing."

"Hell yes. It might sound conceited to say this, but I helped create this scene. Now I'm doing the easier job and letting it destroy itself."

There was truth, as well as conceit, in the statement. The scene had, to a large degree, taken on the flavor of Jerry's wit, of his melancholy, of his abandonment . . . and suddenly, he had left it to its own devices, to its own false gods while he busied himself with more personal matters.

"I created something once," I said. "It wasn't much, but it was interesting. I had a little party, and I arranged lightings and things . . . a red and blue Christmas light. I put on the music I wanted to hear, then sat down and demanded that everyone be quiet and dig it. They were, for a while, then they got restless and sent somebody out for wine, complained about the music. I was put out and decided to destroy it. I turned all the lights back on and put some bad popular music on the phonograph, then left muttering cryptic statements. Everyone wondered what had gotten into me.

"I felt as though I had created a perfect world for them and that they had destroyed it."

"That's the divine pattern. What else could you expect? How can you expect to succeed where God's having the devil's time holding his own?"

I laughed. "It must be damned frustrating to be God."

"It is," Jerry said as though he knew. "The Bible says that God created man in his own image . . . I suppose that meant that he gave him powers of creation too. Take love . . . you can make a girl love you easily enough. That's a form of creation. You just pick her out, say the right things, give her the right looks at the proper times . . . then turn the knob slowly to the right. It works every time, if you use the formula correctly, and it doesn't mean a damned thing. When you get tired of your creation, you just send down a forty-day rain and obliterate it. The whole goddamned thing is so artificial you begin to wonder if there's really any reality.

"You know what the last sound anyone will hear as they blow up the world that was created for them, man?"

"No . . . Screaming?"

"No, God's laughter . . . a good, hearty laugh as the whole damned thing blows to pieces."

"I don't follow you there . . . Only a madman laughs when his plans and creations are destroyed."

"What makes you think that we're the sole extent of creation? I think that the laughter will be something akin to the pleasure you get by picking off a festering scab."

A man who was walking down the opposite side of the street hailed us, "Hey, can you tell me how to get to the freeway?"

"Just keep walking in the direction you're going. You'll come right to it."

"Thanks."

"You know," I said, "we could have told him to go back the way he came and thrown in a couple of right turns. We might have completely changed his fate."

"We might have, if we'd thought of it in time," Jerry laughed. "Hey, Marty told me there was a fountain somewhere along here. Want to look for it?"

We found the fountain on the front lawn of an apartment development. It was a small cement pool with artificial water lilies floating on it. It had a sterile, manufactured look about it, and the spray had been turned off for the night. We looked at it for a while, and I walked around it trying, unsuccessfully, to find the spigot to turn it on.

There was a large wall near the fountain. A bright floodlight shined on it, advertising the name of the development that sheltered the fountain. The wall was elaborately constructed with hundreds of stones, cemented together in a random mosaic. The dark of the night, in combination with the light playing on it, gave the wall a semblance of hundreds of faces squeezed closely together and peering out on the world with hopeless eyes.

I pointed the faces out to Jerry. He looked for a minute. "Pretty wicked-looking crew."

"Maybe . . . not much different from us, though. All of us looking for pretty much the same thing . . . what to believe in a vast colossus of bullshit; truth . . ."

Jerry grimaced. "Think so? Maybe you can tell them about it."

"It wouldn't make any difference if I could, you know. The funny thing about truth is that no matter how obvious it may be, you'll never be able to see it until your mind's ready."

"Maybe it's been ready all along, but it doesn't see truth because truth and the Easter Bunny both live in the same igloo at the North Pole."

"It's not a matter of *seeing* it . . . it's a matter of recognizing it, and it probably takes a lot of practice *recognizing* the big, obvious minor truths in order to spot the small *major* one."

"Or maybe all that practice won't do any good at all . . . Maybe you can recognize an apple at a hundred paces, but that doesn't mean your vision will *ever* be sharp enough to spot the seed."

"There's always the telescope," I answered.

"Yeah, but try to focus the Mount Palomar telescope on a seed a hundred yards from the lens . . . the damned thing's powerful enough to find stars we never knew existed, but it's *too* grandiose and powerful to see anything accurately that's so close to it . . . and the eye's too limited."

"Well then, I guess the easiest thing to do would be to walk the hundred paces, eat the apple, and look at the damned seeds instead of blundering around with the Mount Palomar telescope. Maybe that's what's confusing so many people . . . the same ones who think they need a steam shovel to turn the dirt in a flowerpot."

"The etiquette books might frown on it, but people still have a tendency to spit seeds out if they happen to bite into the core in the first place."

"If they spit them in the right places, they make more seeds, eventually."

"For more people to spit out," he concluded for me.

"Damned cynic," I laughed.

Looming over the top of the wall was a night sky brilliant with stars. The usual evening mist had cleared away, and even the city lights were not bright enough to dull them to any degree.

The constellation Orion was low in the east. "Which one of those stars is Betelgeuse?" I wondered aloud. "I always thought it was the one on the upper left, but the one on the right seems redder."

"Let me use your glasses for a minute. I can't see a damned thing."

He put the glasses on and looked at the winter sky.

"God, how fantastic. I haven't looked at the stars in years." He stood there, his neck craned toward the sky, a wide smile erasing the depression that had etched itself on his face over the last few months. "Man, I can remember when I used to stare at the stars for hours. I always figured I could count on them, and barring clouds, they'd always be there." He continued looking and talking, but not at me. "Great . . . No reason for it, but I suddenly feel completely different than I did before . . . and you *are* still there, aren't you? All of you . . ."

He handed back my glasses, and I looked up again. "Wonder how they keep them up there. By strings, maybe. It's pretty obvious that the sky's an inverted bowl of some kind. You can see it start over there in the east and curve upward and down into the west. Of course, I'd better keep it under my hat . . . Might upset the whole concept of astronomy."

"Yeah, you'd better," he agreed, and we continued walking, saying things of little import and less meaning until we arrived home.

The room was dark, and I stumbled over a National Guard helmet liner, left over from a recent meeting I had attended. I could hear Willy, who had left the party early, snoring peacefully.

I turned on a dim blue light and sat down, putting my helmet on my head while Jerry got ready to sack out.

"What you got there?" he asked, indicating the helmet.

"Oh, just a symbol of the particular group of people I belong to," I answered, "who seek to make the panorama of the stars more perfect for those worlds whose view of the heavens is obstructed by Earth."

"Huh?"

"Never mind," I chuckled. "See you in the morning."

Jerry crawled into bed, but I stayed up thinking for a while, observing the room (along with the Blind Prophet) through the hazy glow created by the dim light and the orange glow of the electric heater.

As my eyes grew accustomed to the light, I could see Willy lying across from me, looking rather peaceful and noble, a victim of the world he tried so hard to love and which kept doing things that weren't at all convivial with his plans for the world as it should be.

A few minutes later, I looked over at Jerry, who had settled down and was lying under a thin blanket and a mangy bathrobe, looking almost like any other human being on Earth, fast away in the domain of sleep.

THINK SLOW AND YOU'RE DEAD . . . THINK FAST AND, EVEN if what spews forth is little more than an idiocy, it keeps conversation at least at babbling point. If it is witty as well, you score points.

Conversation must not cease, or we may each suddenly realize that we have nothing to say.

It was a game, and the "further out" you got, the more you appreciated its subtleties. It was played with a vengeance; its reward: lack of silence . . . introspective silence; silence that nevertheless appeared once good fellowship began wearing thin. A questionable reward at best, but any reward seemed worth striving for as Mecca's shining towers gleam before feet suddenly too tired to journey farther.

After an evening at the "game," I left the bookstore for perhaps the thousandth time. And for the thousandth time, I breathed the silent vow, the vow hoary with age and repetition, the vow to somehow break away. And yet I realized that the sounding board of my mind had become deadened to the familiar syllables. I lit a cigarette. The smoke seemed to burn the roof of my mouth with a bitter-tasting, hot acid. "Christ," I said without much conviction, and threw the scarcely started cigarette on the sidewalk, realizing that it was a luxurious anger I could ill afford but not really giving a damn. I walked a few steps and reconsidered, almost turning around to retrieve the butt, but firmed my resolve and left it lying there . . . a token symbolic of something or other; what, I didn't give a damn.

It was miserable out, even though the night was clear and star speckled. I half wished it would rain so I could find something definite to pin my resentment on. Clenching the zipperless front of my jacket together, I continued walking. My hands started to freeze, but I left them out; feeling a slight satisfaction in the self-inflicted torture.

No one was in the room when I got there. That was good. Disgusting lot anyhow. I lay down on the bed. A vague uneasiness gripped me suddenly. Something was wrong . . . something other than that which occupied my mind. I tried to sleep but found it impossible . . . the uneasiness was insistent and gnawing.

Abruptly, I realized what it was. The bright moonlight flooding through the window cast its light on a blank wall. The Blind Prophet was gone. Had Willy said something about it? I imperfectly remembered that he had. The artist had given the picture to Willy and his ex-girlfriend jointly. The girl had become insistent about ownership rights, and Willy had finally said, "Take the damned thing." That was the last he ever spoke to her that I heard of.

She apparently had taken it, finally, carting it off to New York to grace the wall of her room in the college dorm.

"Well, old buddy," I addressed the blank space on the wall, "I see you've finally split the scene. You always did set a good example. I'll miss you, though."

I pictured the cavernous, sightless eyes, and they almost seemed to reappear on the wall for a moment, aided by the moon-cast shadows, to bid a ghostly "Pick ya up on the next set, partner," then vanished.

Well, I'll be damned, I thought. *He wasn't such a square cat after all.* I laughed silently and closed my eyes.

I WAS WANDERING IDLY THROUGH A WIDE VALLEY, NESTLED AMID stupendous mountains whose peaks jutted out of sight into the deep lapis lazuli sky. A stream coursed leisurely near me, and I unconsciously followed its path as it meandered through emerald fields dotted profusely with tiny flowers of varied brilliant hues. The grass seemed to have been mowed into a velvet-smooth carpet that gave slightly beneath each step, then bounded back again as I moved on, loosing the fresh, pungent smell of grass when it bleeds beneath the mowing blades.

Shimmering stones twinkled at me from the shallow depth of the stream, and I paused to scoop a few of them out. I was disappointed, for they immediately lost their luster, as such stones are wont to do when plucked from their crystal-water womb. I tossed them back in, one at a time, and their untenable sheen mocked me playfully as they settled again beneath the water.

A shadow suddenly fell across them, a human form, blotting out the sweet, dazzling sunlight that lent them a share of its brilliance. I looked up, startled. The shadow seemed to have no owner but rippled across the meadow as far as the eye could see. I began to walk toward it, forsaking the direction offered by the stream. I walked for some time before I made out a vague, titanic form in the distance. Apprehensiveness cautioned me, but I determined to seek the source out, ready to run at any sign of impending danger.

The figure disappeared as I rounded a corner, then sprang into full view not a hundred steps away as I completed the turn. I stopped with a gasp of surprise. It was a woman, but like none ever conceived by human seed. She stood proud and fair, towering an incredible height above me. I crouched back against the corner of stone I had just passed, frightened by her sudden appearance; fascinated by her towering radiance. Her golden, naked skin caught the sunlight . . . seemed alive with it as it glinted off in glistening brilliance.

Her bronze-yellow hair, its fineness not distorted by her immense stature, cascaded in rivulets across her shoulders, whipping in the cool breeze and playing delicately about the firm, muscular taper of her back.

In either hand, she tenderly clasped a fair child. Her eyes, which watched the children she held close to suckle, were of an identical color with the sky. Locks of her fair hair strayed with the whims of the wind across breasts sculptured smooth as fine jade, swelled to exaggerated greatness with the weight of mother's milk, the hair gently whipping and caressing the infants with its bronze strands.

The rock against which I leaned suddenly began to melt away, exposing my presence. I experienced a moment of fear, but if she saw me, she paid no heed.

Her eyes closed, suddenly, and her muscles tightened as though under great tension. A small creature began to emerge from her loins. She caught it as it completed its nativity, and placed it gently on the ground far below. I became aware that there were many others like it crawling about the ground; my fascination with the giantess had kept me from noticing them before. She pulled the two children who were milking her away and placed them on the ground too, then carefully selected two others from the score or more to replace them at the fount. My attention shifted to the children at her feet. Even as I watched, the two children she had just finished nursing began to grow, proud and straight as the giant from which they had generated.

Others crawled, squalling, around them and seemed to shy fearfully away when the soft hand reached down to select those that were to be fed. They seemed misshapen and wizened, their faces fixed in a moronic, drooling stare. The two who had been fed began to circle around the area, curiously inspecting the flowers and strange objects that they found strewn around the ground, but the moronic ones seemed content to shriek alarmingly and crawl about the ground, scarcely moving from the spots where they had been dropped. Piles of filth collected around them through which they moved unheedingly, smearing themselves with the vile dirt.

The colossal mother gently pulled the other two babes from her nipples and placed them on the ground, then began to hunt for another hungry pair. The misshapen creatures on the ground squalled and hissed as her hand approached first one, then another, until finally she stopped searching. The two who had just been fed began to grow rapidly, as had their brothers. Their distaste for the crawling obscenities that were their womb-mates became apparent as they moved off to join the other two in exploring a widening area around their mother.

My eyes traveled back to her face, and suddenly, I noticed deepening wrinkles furrowing her smooth brow. The moronic children on the ground seemed to sense that something was happening and magnified their howling until it became almost unbearable. The bronze hair that still whipped in the wind began to fade until it

189

became the color of the gray clouds that floated heavily through a sky now darkening, eve as the giant's eyes. She made a last attempt to suckle a child, cleaving her hand into the mess of monsters and pulling a protesting brat to her bosom, but too late, for the once bountiful fountains began to sink, and her nipple shriveled from the lax gums of the still-whining, filth-smeared monstrosity.

The straight-boned, fair-skinned children who had been fed at the suddenly declining breast looked on the scene with astonishment . . . then sorrow as crystal tears began to dribble down their rose-petal cheeks. They continued to watch for a while, even as I, then turned about and began to walk slowly in the direction of the hills, first in a group, then dispersing in their own directions. One or another of them would stop occasionally and look back for a few minutes, then, with renewed resolve, continue on his path until disappearing into the distance.

The mother watched her disappearing children until her eyes became heavy and glassy and her body began to sink slowly to the ground, gnarled and wrinkled with sudden age.

The monster children continued their hateful squalling; louder and louder it rose as the once magnificent body of their mother neared the ground. Their thick, crude hands clawed at her thighs, pulling her down with a force her weakened body could not resist.

Then she fell, and the ground trembled as it cushioned the gigantic, suddenly ancient body. The screaming monsters scrambled up the thighs, which began to decompose before my eyes; fighting and clawing at one another in their near frenzy, tearing great hunks from the decaying body as they swarmed over it.

My senses revolted at the spectacle, but I continued to watch, morbidly curious as to what their mission upon the colossal body was to be.

Then, suddenly, I began to understand. The sky darkened perceptibly, and an icy wind swept across the valley, chilling me through.

Each squalling monster had the same hideous objective in mind: that of forcing its gnarled, misshapen, rapidly aging body back into the rotting womb.

A vulture appeared in the sky and began to circle, its red eyes gleaming phosphorescently.

THERE MUST HAVE BEEN THIRTY PEOPLE IN THE BOOKSTORE KICKing the horse, which was bewildering because they all agreed that it was dead; dead because, simply enough, it was no longer alive . . . and yet they were intent on reviving it, forcing pure, sweet air into lungs filled with soot and tied off with a golden chain.

"Scene, scene!" the parched cry arose, and yet the "scene" did not come, for the "scene" is not a *now* thing but a stew blending out of the past. The "scene" is *always* in the past, and only by subtly combining the past with the present and future until they all merge into a vast out-of-time plane can it be appreciated.

There is a plaintive country tune which bewails the fact that:

All the good times are past and gone,
All the good times are o'er,
All the good times are past and gone,
Little darlin', don't weep no more.

It comes from the same melancholy world as the White Queen's jam: "Jam yesterday and jam tomorrow, but never jam today." One hopes for the jams that are still to come; one remembers the jams that first whetted the taste. One longs for past jams while tasting present jams and longing for future jams, sometimes becoming so engrossed in the contemplation of vicissitude that one never tastes the sweetness that lies thickly spread over the bread of now.

I HAD BEEN SITTING IN THE BOOKSTORE SINCE THREE IN THE afternoon watching people filter in, each wondering where the party was going to be since it was, after all, a Friday night. And when they had all gathered . . . talking, singing, and looking as though they were enjoying themselves, they were still wondering where it was going to be. Later in the evening, several of them went to check over the coffeehouse, where Marty, the school-teacher, suddenly loosed twenty-six years of pent-up frustrations by punching the proprietor in the belly after exchanging a few sour remarks. After a week of talking about nothing else, it looked as though this had been the ultimate purpose of his existence, his kismet. Born and raised in Brooklyn, an MA in English, five hundred pages of poetry that no one appreciated, and several years of teaching high school kids who didn't give a damn . . . all of this went into the proprietor's well-rounded expanse of stomach. He hit Marty back, so Marty left driving a new Lambretta scooter, determined to take a trip around the world. What else was there to do? (Several months later, I received a letter postmarked "Brooklyn, NY." He had gotten as far as Acapulco, sold his scooter, and hitchhiked back to Brooklyn. His mother and his brother were both doing fine.)

Jerry, attired in his now omnipresent suit, came in lugging his monstrous guitar case. No one had ever believed it would happen, least of all Jerry. He had spent a month's wages on a new custom guitar with a velvet-lined case big enough to bury both of them in.

I sat next to Barbara while Jerry tuned up his guitar. I found myself saying unimportant things with hidden meanings and wondering why there was a wall where there had once been a "love scene."

I secretly drank cola-flavored gin from a paper cup as, between snatches of polite conversation, I sized up the walls. I suddenly began to see a definite substance to them. They were walls of reason and rationality that a person can build around himself without even being aware of the process. I began to wonder why I hadn't been capable of perceiving these walls before. The answer was forthcoming and unavoidable: my *own* walls were partially blinding my view.

The walls were assembled brick by brick, and when the masonry is finished, the builder suffocates. It comes as a surprise, for it doesn't take as long as might be thought to finish the job with an able, though perverted Fortunato pitching in to swiftly and efficiently seal his own tomb.

Jerry sang, the tones of his bright new guitar rippling against the bricks not yet dry . . . but drying; the mortar becoming one with the brick upon brick, which mounted to banish the light and stagnate the air.

"I feel like a cigar!" Barbara suddenly announced (Barbara always "announced" things of this nature), breaking through my reverie.

"A what?"

"Cigar . . . Let's go." And before I had time to protest, I was lured out the door into the cold night air in search of a cigar store.

She decided not to smoke the cigar once I had bought it, so I lit it myself as we walked the five blocks back to the bookstore.

We walked the first two blocks in silence while I awaited whatever inquisition was to come. Barbara's ruses were predictable.

"You don't look in very high spirits," she began at last.

"I'm not . . . I guess," I answered, on my guard.

"Want to talk about it?"

"I would, but I don't quite know how . . . It involves a lot of personal hang-ups you wouldn't understand."

Telling a woman she might not understand your problems (especially if it's Barbara) is a fatal flaw if one wishes to keep one's hassles to one's self.

"Try me."

"Later," I answered, "I promise."

We half listened to the music and were half-enveloped in our personal worlds as the evening rolled on. The music, however, seemed to be the more powerful force. I got up and put on my jacket.

"Where to?" Barbara asked.

"I think I'll go out and look at stars for a while."

"I'll come out in a few minutes too," she said.

I walked out to the parking lot and sat down on the railing. There were no stars. The sky had a pink overcast to it, the reflected glory of an infinity of neon signs, captured in the haze and reaching to the very ceiling of the earth. I looked skyward for a while, then rested my head on my arms. Footsteps clicked across the lot, but I didn't look up until they stopped in front of me.

"Hi, Karen."

"Are you all right?" she asked uncertainly.

Karen was the guardian angel of my moods (self-appointed) whose main mission in life, or so it seemed to me, was to tell me to smile and not look so depressed all the time. Nothing depressed me quite so much as being told not to be depressed when I damned well *felt* like being depressed.

"Nothing. S'fine. I was just watching the stars."

She looked at the overcast sky, then cocked a suspicious eyebrow at me. Barbara suddenly appeared around the corner, balancing herself along the rail.

"Well, I'll leave you in charge of the cheering-up committee," Karen said to her, winked, then escaped back into the bookstore.

Barbara sat down beside me. "As honorary chairman of the good-cheer committee, I've been advised . . ."

"Maintain, wench. I'm enjoying my misery, all of which tends to make me slightly sadistic . . . I pass it along for others to enjoy." She touched my arm and looked serious.

"If you ever hear anybody call me selfish," I continued, "just send him around when I'm 'down.' Share? I mean to tell you, I'll knock him over. Hand him a shovel and tell him to dig right into the pile . . . take all he can carry."

Barbara was silent for a moment. She held her head in her hands and toyed with a loose strand of hair. "It's a full pile, though," she said finally. "The more people you set to working on it, the longer it takes to flatten the ground. Besides, they all have piles of their own to take care of. You're likely to turn around one of these days and notice some of them throwing *their* dirt on *your* pile. Misery loves company, but not company with more misery. There! I made an epigram . . ."

"Then why do you want in on mine, coming out here?"

"Oh . . . maybe because I suspect my pile might be on the same ground as yours . . . if mine really even exists. I'm not sure, but I sense it, and it makes me uneasy."

"For God's sake, Barb, don't go looking for problems. Let *them* hunt *you* out . . . They'll be around soon enough anyway. Hell, you might even be lucky . . . You might walk around with a brass ring on your finger for the rest of your life, thinking it's gold . . . and it might just as well *be* gold, since you believe it is. Why should I come up and tell you it isn't, because it looks like mine, and I know damned well what mine's made of?"

"Because I might try to pawn it someday and find out it's worth nothing."

"I guess you might at that. But hell, who knows . . . All the 'gold' rings in the world may be made of the same junk. Not very many people ever *try* to cash them in. They might be better off being spared the disillusionment altogether."

"What about the ones who *suspect* but don't know? Neither the happy people nor the disillusioned ones have any cause to worry . . . They either know the answer or else think they do . . . and that frees them in a way. The ones who aren't sure one way or another, they're the ones who keep the sleeping pill companies in business."

"They're also the ones who leave things when they move on while the others just move along. They're the ones who turn into Rimbauds and Beethovens. The others illustrate comic books or torture cats."

"You're trying to get me off the point, Bob. We both know that whatever's on your mind isn't going to open the ground, à la *Faust*, and swallow me."

"I know," I admitted. "The only reason I'm beating around the bush is so you'll talk to me for a while. To tell the truth, I can't put my finger on whatever it is, or I would have taken care of it long ago."

"Well, what does it *feel* like, then?"

"I dunno . . . it's an uneasy kind of thing that's been on my back for months. Maybe it's the scene, such as it is . . . or maybe it's me."

"They're the same animal in any case. It boils down to you, right?"

"Right, Dr. Freud," I laughed. "But it's convenient to hang it on something else. Saves facing the issue."

"Saves *solving* it too, Dr. Watson."

"Maybe that's where the hang-up is. I've been sitting around the bookstore waiting for it to solve itself, but it suddenly is becoming apparent that it doesn't intend to do any such thing."

"Check me if I'm wrong, Bob, but I think you've just struck oil. The key word is *bookstore*, and the verb is *sitting*."

"I thought verbs were words denoting action. Hell, Barb, I've thought of that angle until it's coming out my ear."

"Correct . . . Right on the button, in fact. You've told me about it before . . . and you know *where*?"

I answered rather weakly, for it was a rather weak answer: "Sitting . . . in the bookstore."

She had the ball suddenly, and she wasn't about to let it drop. "It's a bad scene, Bob. A *very* bad scene. It's called *apathy*, and it's a heck of a lot better to be miserable than apathetic. You can get rid of something that really hurts you, when you set your mind to it, but apathy hangs *on* because it makes you not care enough to even bother looking for a way out."

I started to answer, but my voice caught in my throat, so I nodded.

"I feel it too, so don't think you're the Lone Ranger. Sometimes it scares me when I suddenly wake up and realize how far it's gotten . . . and I start thinking about things . . . like the time we went up to the castle and that poem you wrote about it for my birth present . . . I still have it, by the way . . . and a lot of other things, hundreds of them. Then I begin to wonder why we don't do these things anymore . . . we haven't for a long time, you know. It's this *damned* apathy, and I begin to hate it so much I cry. I do that every once in a while. It convinces me that I still know how to feel things. I *need* convincing because I sometimes wonder if there's really anything there anymore."

She shoved her hands into her coat pockets and said nothing for a while. I wanted to comfort her and tell her that it was all right and that there really wasn't any apathy. For a faltering moment, I wanted to tell it to myself as well, to renew my waning faith in the false comforter . . . the comforter with the clouded eye and the deadened senses, the lukewarm blood.

Then something began to happen. It began to get stronger and stronger . . . It was like the tingle of blood that courses through your veins as you thaw your hands over a hot woodstove while an icy wind rattles at the windows that look out over the frosted landscape of a very cold winter. It was this and yet mental.

I started talking about walls, the scene, and whatever happened to spurt through my mind. Barbara pushed her hands deeper into her pockets and listened, though not entirely. A vague discontent seemed to emanate from her.

"Jerry still singing in there?" she asked suddenly.

"I don't know. I guess so." I looked at her oddly for a brief moment; she looked away and shoved her hands deeper still into the pockets.

"I'll be damned," I mumbled, and tried not to smile. She didn't answer.

Jerry appeared, wandering around the side of the building. He looked at us, his eyes not seeming to quite focus.

"Cold out here," he observed to the parking lot.

"I know," I answered.

"What are you trying to do, freeze?"

"No. We're watching the stars, only there aren't any. Join us?"

"No thanks." He turned around and lit a cigarette, then started walking back to the bookstore.

"Why?" Barbara said softly, watching Jerry go back in.

"I don't know, Barb . . . Maybe he . . . I don't know. I doubt if *he* does."

We sat there awhile longer, silently, then went back inside. Jerry stood, tie loosened, continuing his show. The lights had been repaired (they'd been on the blink for months), and the room was brightly lit. It looked strange; the whole atmosphere seemed changed and somehow wrong. I looked around at the faces that were rather vacantly watching Jerry perform.

There were a few faces I didn't recognize and some I knew only slightly, sitting at the long, black table. I felt a slight irritation; that was *our* table . . . the table around which, every night that nothing else was happening, were grouped "us." But it wasn't "us" at the table tonight, nor was it "us" who had made the party scene for the last couple of months.

A few of the "old" faces were there, and, as I looked them over, they seemed somehow different from the "new" faces . . . a little older and more introspective, but with the same subtle bewilderment behind the eyes. It seemed to have left a permanent stamp, a sort of physical-psychological "fraternity pin" on the "old" faces.

199

I wondered if I had it. I wasn't sure . . . I'd never noticed it if I did . . . but, then, I'd never noticed it on them before, either.

I glanced at Barbara to see if she had followed the route my eyes had traced across the room. She was watching Jerry intently.

I looked back at the table. The conversation was being monopolized by a rather offbeat-looking boy with a thin blond beard. I watched the looks of unabashed admiration turned upon him by his group and wondered how long the full cycle took. I could taste a salty smile on my lips as I turned away again.

"Go, man, go," I whispered inaudibly. "It's a great game."

I tore open an empty cigarette pack and wrote on it, then handed it to Barbara. She read it and smiled. "Can I keep?"

"Sure. Not very original, even as a quote, I'm afraid."

Jerry finished his song and put his guitar in the case, tenderly tucking it into its velvet crib and snapping its numerous fastenings. The ceremony completed, he came over to our table and pulled up a chair. He sat rigidly, his hands ill at ease on the tabletop. "Like some coffee, Barb?"

"Hmm? Oh, no thanks, Jer."

He sat still for a few minutes more, a growing tension evident on his face. It finally broke. "Well, let's have it. There's something the matter with you people . . ."

Barbara pushed the penciled cigarette package toward him. He didn't seem to notice it.

"Bob, have you been drinking or something? You shouldn't. You make a fool out of yourself. And what's up with you, Barb . . ."

"It's right under your nose, Jer," I said.

He picked up the paper and read it, then put it down and looked me in the eye with a "what are you trying to prove?" look. "Did it take Keats to tell you that?"

I didn't answer. I thought of things to say, but they were better said with silence. He looked at the paper again, then suddenly grinned. I could feel a chink falling out of the wall.

Beauty is truth, truth beauty,
—that is all
Ye know on earth, and all ye need to know.

I got up and walked outside. I didn't know where I was going or exactly why except that I had a feeling of suddenly being cut off from a warm, secure nothingness and forced out into a harsh, cold fascination. The door over which I had pondered so long was flung open, and there was no return . . . no turning back as it slammed and bolted emphatically.

Barbara followed. We met in the parking lot.

I grinned at her, not finding nor requiring any words to communicate that which cannot, after all, be conveyed in speech.

"Hey," I said suddenly. "Feel like running around the block?"

"Why not!"

Jerry came out, his earlier questions still, apparently, unanswered. "Look, something's up. What in hell's going on?"

"Nothing much."

"Now look, we've been sitting around in there bum-kicking the hell out of one another . . . There must be some reason for it."

Barbara smiled. "How'd you like to run around the block with us?"

Jerry was somewhat taken aback. Obviously, no one was going to answer a simple, straightforward question. He looked grave for a moment, as though he doubted our collective sanity. The three of us stood there; Barbara and I waited. A fine line seemed to play

201

for an instance between Jerry's eyebrows as though a loose wire were trying to decide the proper circuit with which to join. Then, suddenly, he grinned and screwed one eye off to the side . . . "Why not?"

"Hey, look," Barbara announced, "the stars are finally out." The overcast had rolled away, and a few brave stars had, indeed, managed to poke through the mist.

I started running. There was a slight hesitation behind me, then running steps.

"Hey, not so fast! I have heels on!" Barbara shouted. Jerry had already caught up with me, so we slowed down to let Barbara pull ahead, then swooped past her again. Jerry caught her hand, pulling her on faster until she broke away to pick a potted gardenia off a lawn. "Catch!" She threw the pot to Jerry, who ran a few steps with it and passed it on to me with a loud out-of-breath laugh.

There was a thickening mist in the air that suddenly turned into a light, pattering rain since it was, after all, nearing winter.

THAT WHICH GOES UP MUST COME DOWN, AND THAT which is born must someday die. And so the scene disintegrated. There was nothing spectacular about it; it had begun to crumble at the foundations and slowly moldered to the ground. It ended as it had begun: with a party.

I have a keen recollection of the party, for I sat in the corner on a pile of orange and yellow cushions and watched. I had an old notebook open, writing down things that I wanted to remember, for I knew that I would never again see any of these people quite the way I saw them that night.

It was a small party, a farewell to Alan, who had completed his sojourn in the "colonies" and was getting ready to go back to England and prepare for a long, studious year at Cambridge. Alan had arrived at the beginning of the "scene" and was, I suspect, the catalyst of the affair. He had come, infecting those he encountered and was close to with a keen perception of things as they are (or, more properly, as they should be), which was the indispensable element in whatever strange ambrosia it was that we had concocted.

The scene was played, and the principals were ready to make their exits. Alan was ready to sail, his suitcases packed and the few things he couldn't squeeze in them distributed to his needier compatriots.

John was packed too. He had decided, "Well, when Alan splits, I guess I'll make it somewhere too. Probably won't be much left around here in the way of a scene." His small backpack of essential "road" equipment sat in the corner (he was the only "dude" in the world who considered hair oil to be an essential; it was his own blend, which he used once a week to control his unwieldy profusion of hair) ready to sustain him wherever he might go upon the nation's steel-railed commerce veins . . . to Denver, New York, or Mississippi . . . it was all the same; some place to go and some place to come back to . . .

Jerry, feeling the loss of his comrades, was ready to go as well, although not by boat or freight. His mode of transportation was indefinite and his direction "God knows where," a place of mind to which he alone knew the directions.

I, too, knew that the climax had been reached. That was why I had the notebook open, scribbling down impressions and snatches of conversation.

The talk of the evening was tinted with wine; the wine that dulls the reservations and sharpens the emotions. The wine that nullifies the sophistication and reawakens the wonder of each moment of living; that has a truth of its own, untainted by the logical mind; a truth that is true because it is *felt* to be rather than reasoned.

In the course of the evening, Jerry had come up with a definition of living, which I immediately jotted down in my notebook.

"I'll tell you what living is," he had said. "It's a maze . . . only you don't see it from the top like a picture, and you aren't given a pencil to trace out the path with. You're in it . . . and every so often, you come to dead ends."

"I know, man," John said. "That's where I am right now. So where do I go from there?"

"Well, to begin with, you sit there for a while not knowing what to do, since you've been all over the damned thing already looking for a way out. Then you see a flaw in the wall, not a very big one, but you can see light on the other side, and so you decide to quit following the rules and you tear and rip at the flaw until you get through. And you know what's on the other side?"

"Hell yes, man," John answered fatalistically. "Another dead end if it's the same maze I'm thinking about."

"Exactly, exactly," Jerry said enthusiastically. "But a dead end with another flaw in it, man, another wall to tear away at until you get through . . ."

"To another dead end. A weird way to get your kicks if you ask me . . ."

"You're saying that the ultimate goal in life is to find another goal," I said. "What happens when there are no more goals?"

Jerry was ready for the question. "You die, of course . . . suddenly."

"And maybe that's only the beginning," Alan added.

"Even so, it's a damned fatalistic approach to life, isn't it?"

"No, there's more to it than that . . . there's little side paths all along. That's where we are right now, see? There's everything in that maze . . . scenes, people, parties . . . The thing is to forget it's a maze except when it comes right up and tells you so; the secret's in accepting the fact, then forgetting it. See?"

"Hey, man," John interjected. He had been working on his notebook for some time, giggling occasionally. "I've got it . . . the perfect social situation."

"Uh-oh . . . Here we go on another one of John's trips," Jerry said.

"Wait, dig this. First we elect Ferlinghetti mayor of San Francisco, see? Then we get on his committee and talk him into seceding from the Union . . ."

"Oh yeah?" Jerry said. "Just how do you plan to go about—"

"Later, man, later." John waved him off frantically. "Don't hassle me with hassles right now. We can work over the small points later. Now, we raise ourselves an army down on North Beach . . . that should be easy enough . . . then we march down to Big Sur, taking over everything on the way."

"What are you planning to do once you get that far?" I asked naïvely.

"Oh, man, are you kidding me? What am I going to do? I'll tell you what I'm going to do . . . I'm going to *burn* everything, man . . . everything except a couple of hotels, then clear the land off for agriculture."

"Agriculture?"

"Hoo boy . . . the agriculture center of the *world*. The main and only product to be raised, imported, and exported will be *weed*, man. I can see it now . . . farmers giggling to market with truckloads of joints, being paid with the same stuff, and 'tripping' back again. I'll make it a legal offense not to be blasted. Of course, I realize that it'd be completely impractical economics-wise, but who'd care?"

And so the night went on, and at dawn, we drove up to Twin Peaks to watch the sunrise over San Francisco. The sunrise was completely lost that day in the fog, which rolled in from the bay, cleansing the city for another hard day of play in the colossal playground.

We watched the blocks of streetlights flick off across the holy city as it began to come to life. Alan watched pensively, lost in thought. A smile would begin to form every once in a while, but was brushed away by a look of lingering sadness. All was silence in the gray heaviness of the dawn, and then we pulled away and drove down the pale streets back to the apartment.

Jerry sat next to the window and watched the mist-shrouded houses whisk by until his eyes closed. He began to snore faintly, and his head dropped to John's shoulder. John looked down at him, not quite knowing what to make of the whole thing, then chuckled silently and looked out the window, clasping and unclasping his fingers in his perpetual nervousness.

I caught Alan's eye in the rearview mirror. I winked at him. He turned around and surveyed the three of us in the back seat with a gentle, all-encompassing smile. "Wow . . . ," he said finally. "Wow . . ." A word that carried a complex of emotions and associations in its simplicity. Then he turned around and stretched an arm over the back of the seat. His head nodded slightly, but his eyes stayed open, unwilling to let any of the vague kaleidoscope slip by unnoticed.

Slowly, his mood pervaded the car, a warm sort of nonverbal fascination flavored with the taste of many days and nights . . . and a comforting realization. It was nothing that needed to be talked about this time. We had talked about it before, so now we knew, and were silent with our knowledge. The love scene had seen fit to reappear for a few moments, that was all. Only this time, there was no talk, no heralds, no sense of tingling anticipation surrounding her visit.

On a morning in San Francisco, after a small party, traveling down an unfamiliar street at early dawn, she had found us, and she looked the same as always.

Her eyes dim and missing many faults; her mind that of a very young child, unspoiled by such coarse things as knowledge and reality, believing unquestioningly in beauty and justness. Her elusive hand is soft and shy and must be sought with truth and understanding.

Her tears are gentle tears and sweeten the heart with memories of times since fled but never quite forgotten.

Her partings are painful and unpredictable, and when she is gone, one waits . . . one waits, not really even knowing what it is one waits for, but one waits if only because her faint scent lingers about all who have breathed of her breath and been touched by her soul.

AFTERWORD
—BY BRIGID MEIER—

I N LATE MAY 1961, ROBERT HUNTER, THEN NINETEEN YEARS old, gave me the following poem as a birthday present:

For Barbara
In the pale land of remembered youth
Sleeps a wonderland of miniature joys,
Where love lingers mistily in castles since deserted
Amidst sweet nectars tasted and never quite forgotten.

Through a gently clouded mind there lingers
A land of softly painted passions,
of leaping and crying and twelve-string guitars,
and home by five o'clock (except when one feels otherwise)

Of misty days and sunshine love,
Where inspiration is a light in the wood
Filtering softly through the trees
on a spring afternoon.

'Tis a land where one huddled
In exquisite fear of two-legged monsters
with clouded eye
Who cannot remember when,
Except now and again.

A land where soupbones become roasts,
although I've promised not to tell,
and one waited in half-expectations of woodland nymphs
In a never-quite-forgotten garden.

For anyone familiar with Robert Hunter's prodigious oeuvre as a foremost American lyricist for over fifty years, this early poem is instantly recognizable. All the signature iconic Hunter tropes of romantic gardens and ethereal memories spiced with specific details culled from daily life like twelve-string guitars and soupbones could, if set to music, slip easily into his extensive songbook. I had offered the at-the-time penniless, often-ravenous Hunter a roast beef sandwich in exchange for a ride home, but it turned out I had overestimated how much meat there was—my mother had planned to make soup from the leftovers—and I suspect Bob had to make do with a bowl of cornflakes. He teased me about my miscalculation for a long time.

Robert Hunter's memoir / novella / creative nonfiction *The Silver Snarling Trumpet* was also first written in real time in 1961 as it was happening, a log of events strung together in a narrative or journal of an era the author intuitively knew, despite his youth, was singularly unique. In the year following those events, he curated and edited his text, adding in flourishes of philosophy from the vantage point of hindsight. Back then, he claimed he was "working on a novel," a creative endeavor that became a container from which he evolved his identity as an adult while simultaneously honing his craft as a writer.

Twenty years later, Bob reread his writing and offered commentary as a wiser, successful author and songwriter. Then he put the manuscript in a trunk, placed the trunk in a storage locker for forty years, from where it was recently retrieved by his widow and literary executor, Maureen Hunter. *The Silver Snarling Trumpet* is a rare historical find, a time capsule glimpse of a pivot point in what is broadly known as the counterculture. Robert Hunter captured an amorphous juncture, a hitherto undocumented missing link between the Beat generation literary movement (that itself arose from an older bohemianism that was then augmented with existentialism and informed by jazz) and what later became known as the hippie revolution of the late 1960s. In between, there was a transitional gap of empty space or a generative creative cauldron of pure potentiality for which there is no defining label. We who lived it called it "the thing" or "the scene," as there was no reference point to describe what we were experiencing. We knew *something* was happening, and Bob Hunter was prescient enough to get it down on paper as it unfolded.

I met Robert Hunter, Jerry Garcia, and Alan Trist (who were each under twenty years old) in March 1961, when I was fifteen and still in high school. They had only recently met, and somehow we four bonded and became inseparable for many months. They would pick me up after class, or we would meet at nearby Kepler's Books, where, fueled by coffee, we would proceed to rave. Despite the Beat movement having already peaked, we might have been mistaken for teenage baby beatniks. We were each voracious readers, precocious budding intellectuals, and pretentious artists and poets. And we each had a healthy dose of rabid antiauthoritarianism combined with a sense of the absurd; we knew we didn't belong to the dominant culture of consumerism and conformity, so we created our own culture simply by being friends and allowing that circle of friendship to expand organically. If you thought you were one of us, you were welcome to join in.

> *He speaks of angels and snowy hillsides*
> *But I am rapture of the thing*
> *where we are all in love*
> *with Life*
> *and each other*
>
> *Never before and perhaps again*
> *will it be so*
> *with such youthful vigor*
> *and wild eyes*
>
> *He who creates such beautiful music*
> *radiates it upon us*
> *The one of poetic words encourages*
> *and overwhelms us with faith*
>
> *The blind man in the corner sees all*
> *even though he believes not in himself today*
> *And I, follower of each,*
> *cry beautiful tears of joy.*

Such were my sentiments enshrined in my sophomoric poem written in the spring of 1961—a heartfelt expression of what it felt like to be adored and included by three older, worldlier, and more talented creatives. Jerry is of course the musician, Alan the poet, and Bob the blind man by virtue of his glasses. The "he" in the beginning line refers to poet Kenneth Patchen, who lived in Menlo Park, whom we would visit on occasion.

The scene was intensely literary. But also extremely silly. Bob's verbatim transcription of an extended riff between Alan and Jerry wherein they describe their probably never-written-down theatrical "play" is one long digression of ever-expanding, outlandish alliteration that Bob eerily captures with pitch-perfect accuracy. We did not take ourselves seriously, and we were eager to undermine and poke fun at any and all pomposity. There was a Monty Python–esque quality to whatever pattern interrupts we indulged in to cut through the solid, pervading political and cultural grimness. The "holy goof" immortalized by Kerouac became our unspoken Zen lunatic inspiration. Years later, with the infusion of LSD, it was turbocharged and embraced as the Merry Pranksters' fundamental ethos.

But in 1961/62, we had no drugs, so spontaneous dada zaniness was highly prized as a "high," hence the running-around-the-block incident toward the end of the book. The point was to laugh at it all. James Joyce's *Finnegans Wake* and Lewis Carroll's *Jabberwocky* were among our prime texts, which, when read aloud, could, while being extrapolated upon, reduce us all to puddles of hilarity. We would keep the verbal improvisation going just to see how far over the top we could stand the wordplay before our stomachs ached from too much laughing. We generated our own endogenous drugs—serotonin, dopamine, and oxytocin—from singing and laughing and bonding as a gang of close-knit misfit friends.

My sixteenth birthday party was on May 26, 1961, and I invited the whole Kepler's crowd. My mother barbecued hamburgers on the back patio, and my father brought home a Wollensak reel-to-reel recorder from his work at Stanford Research Institute to tape Bob and Jerry leading us in a sing-along made up of Weavers folk songs and Kingston Trio hits. My father welcomed my newfound ragtag friends, but he was at a loss to understand what I saw in them. Regarding Jerry, to whom he gave some of his Big Bill Broonzy 78s, he said, "He's just a bum—he'll never amount to anything."

My father did live to see Jerry become successful, but how could he have ever imagined that the music Jerry and Robert Hunter penned together would thrive to this day? Or that the spirit of community that engendered that music continues to flourish among their millions of fans? Woven from many eclectic strands of Americana, traditional folklore and folk music, literary and lowbrow references, Robert Hunter's songs became breadcrumbs of wisdom to follow, teachings to learn from, the beloved anthems of several generations. If you listen closely, you can hear the joy (that once made me cry "beautiful tears") come through as the faint high notes of a silver trumpet that long ago let go of snarling and evolved into a Pied Piper's clarion call to laugh and live—yes, joyfully—in the present moment. It's always there if you have ears to hear. Robert Hunter heard loud and clear before almost any of us and well enough to show the way forward through the lyrics of his songs.